50 Family Favorite Dishes
Recipes for Home

By: Kelly Johnson

Table of Contents

- Spaghetti and meatballs
- Roast chicken
- Lasagna
- Beef stew
- Macaroni and cheese
- Chicken pot pie
- Meatloaf
- Tacos
- Shepherd's pie
- Baked ziti
- Pulled pork sandwiches
- Chili
- Chicken parmigiana
- Beef stir-fry
- BBQ ribs
- Fish tacos
- Stuffed peppers
- Shrimp scampi
- Veggie stir-fry
- Chicken fajitas
- Beef burritos
- Ratatouille
- Pad Thai
- Beef Wellington
- Chicken tikka masala
- Eggplant Parmesan
- Beef enchiladas
- Baked salmon
- Jambalaya
- Swedish meatballs
- Stuffed cabbage rolls
- Chicken curry
- Paella
- Beef kebabs
- Egg fried rice
- Chicken noodle soup

- Goulash
- Stuffed mushrooms
- Lemon garlic butter shrimp
- Baked potato soup
- Pork schnitzel
- Teriyaki chicken
- Spanakopita
- Cornbread
- Quiche Lorraine
- Beef pot pie
- Ceviche
- Chicken and dumplings
- Beef lasagna
- Cauliflower cheese

Spaghetti and meatballs

Ingredients:

- Spaghetti pasta
- Meatballs (made from ground beef, breadcrumbs, Parmesan cheese, eggs, and seasoning)
- Tomato sauce (often with garlic, onions, tomatoes, herbs like basil and oregano, and sometimes red wine)
- Grated Parmesan cheese (for topping)
- Fresh basil or parsley (optional, for garnish)

Instructions:

1. Cook the spaghetti pasta according to package instructions until al dente. Drain and set aside.
2. While the pasta is cooking, prepare the meatballs by combining ground beef, breadcrumbs, Parmesan cheese, eggs, salt, pepper, and any other desired seasonings in a bowl. Roll into meatballs about 1-1.5 inches in diameter.
3. In a large skillet or saucepan, heat olive oil over medium heat. Add minced garlic and chopped onions, cooking until softened and fragrant.
4. Add the tomato sauce to the skillet. Season with salt, pepper, dried basil, dried oregano, and a pinch of sugar (if desired) to balance the acidity of the tomatoes. You can also add a splash of red wine for depth of flavor.
5. Gently place the meatballs into the simmering sauce. Cover and let them cook for about 15-20 minutes, or until they are cooked through.
6. Once the meatballs are cooked, carefully transfer them to a plate. Add the cooked spaghetti to the skillet with the tomato sauce, tossing to coat the pasta evenly.
7. Serve the spaghetti topped with the meatballs, additional sauce, and a generous sprinkle of grated Parmesan cheese.
8. Garnish with fresh basil or parsley if desired, and serve hot.

Enjoy this comforting and delicious spaghetti and meatballs dish with your family!

Roast chicken

Ingredients:

- 1 whole chicken (about 3-4 pounds)
- 2-3 tablespoons olive oil or melted butter
- Salt and pepper
- Optional: herbs like rosemary, thyme, or sage (fresh or dried)
- Optional: garlic cloves, lemon wedges, or onion slices for stuffing

Instructions:

1. Preheat your oven to 400°F (200°C).
2. Remove the chicken from packaging and pat dry with paper towels. This helps the skin crisp up during roasting.
3. Place the chicken in a roasting pan or baking dish. If desired, stuff the cavity with herbs, garlic, lemon, or onion slices for added flavor.
4. Rub the chicken all over with olive oil or melted butter. This helps the skin brown nicely and keeps the meat moist.
5. Season the chicken generously with salt and pepper, both inside the cavity and on the outside skin. If using herbs, sprinkle them over the chicken as well.
6. Tie the legs together with kitchen twine if desired (this helps the chicken cook evenly).
7. Place the roasting pan with the chicken in the preheated oven. Roast for about 1 hour and 15 minutes to 1 hour and 30 minutes, or until the internal temperature of the thickest part of the thigh reaches 165°F (75°C) when tested with a meat thermometer.
8. Baste the chicken occasionally with the pan juices or melted butter throughout the cooking process to keep it moist and flavorful.
9. Once done, remove the chicken from the oven and let it rest for about 10-15 minutes before carving. This allows the juices to redistribute throughout the meat.
10. Carve the chicken into serving pieces and arrange on a platter. Serve with your favorite side dishes like roasted vegetables, mashed potatoes, or a fresh salad.

Enjoy your homemade roast chicken with your family!

Lasagna

Ingredients:

- 1 pound (450g) lasagna noodles (oven-ready or boiled according to package instructions)
- 1 pound (450g) ground beef (or a combination of beef and pork)
- 1 onion, finely chopped
- 3 cloves garlic, minced
- 1 can (28 oz or 800g) crushed tomatoes
- 1 can (6 oz or 170g) tomato paste
- 1 cup (240ml) water or beef broth
- 2 teaspoons dried basil
- 1 teaspoon dried oregano
- Salt and pepper to taste
- 15 oz (425g) ricotta cheese
- 1 egg
- 1/2 cup (50g) grated Parmesan cheese
- 2 cups (200g) shredded mozzarella cheese
- Fresh basil or parsley, chopped (optional, for garnish)

Instructions:

1. Preheat your oven to 375°F (190°C).
2. In a large skillet or saucepan, cook the ground beef over medium heat until browned. Add the chopped onion and minced garlic, cooking until the onion is translucent and fragrant.
3. Stir in the crushed tomatoes, tomato paste, water or beef broth, dried basil, dried oregano, salt, and pepper. Bring to a simmer and let it cook for about 10-15 minutes, stirring occasionally. Adjust seasoning to taste.
4. In a bowl, mix together the ricotta cheese, egg, and grated Parmesan cheese until well combined.
5. To assemble the lasagna, spread a thin layer of the meat sauce on the bottom of a 9x13 inch baking dish. Arrange a single layer of lasagna noodles over the sauce. Spread about one-third of the ricotta mixture evenly over the noodles. Top with one-third of the shredded mozzarella cheese. Repeat these layers (sauce, noodles, ricotta mixture, mozzarella) two more times, ending with a final layer of noodles topped with sauce and mozzarella cheese.
6. Cover the baking dish with aluminum foil, tenting it slightly to prevent the cheese from sticking.
7. Bake in the preheated oven for 45 minutes. Then, remove the foil and bake for an additional 10-15 minutes, or until the cheese is bubbly and lightly browned.
8. Remove the lasagna from the oven and let it rest for 10 minutes before slicing and serving. Garnish with chopped fresh basil or parsley if desired.

9. Serve warm and enjoy the delicious layers of homemade lasagna with your family and friends!

This lasagna recipe can be customized by adding vegetables like spinach or mushrooms, or by using different types of cheeses to suit your taste. It's a comforting dish that's perfect for gatherings or a cozy family dinner.

Beef stew

Ingredients:

- 2 pounds (about 1 kg) beef chuck roast, cut into 1-inch cubes
- Salt and pepper
- 1/4 cup all-purpose flour
- 3 tablespoons olive oil or vegetable oil, divided
- 1 onion, chopped
- 3 cloves garlic, minced
- 4 cups beef broth
- 1 cup red wine (optional, can substitute with more beef broth)
- 2 tablespoons tomato paste
- 1 teaspoon Worcestershire sauce
- 1 teaspoon dried thyme
- 2 bay leaves
- 4 carrots, peeled and cut into 1-inch chunks
- 3-4 potatoes, peeled and cut into 1-inch chunks
- 1 cup frozen peas (optional)
- Chopped fresh parsley, for garnish (optional)

Instructions:

1. Season the beef cubes generously with salt and pepper. Place them in a large bowl and toss with the flour until evenly coated.
2. In a large pot or Dutch oven, heat 2 tablespoons of oil over medium-high heat. Working in batches, brown the beef cubes on all sides. Transfer the browned beef to a plate and set aside.
3. Add the remaining 1 tablespoon of oil to the pot. Add the chopped onion and cook until softened, about 5 minutes. Add the minced garlic and cook for another minute until fragrant.
4. Pour in the beef broth and red wine (if using), scraping the bottom of the pot to loosen any browned bits. Stir in the tomato paste, Worcestershire sauce, dried thyme, and bay leaves.
5. Return the browned beef and any accumulated juices to the pot. Bring the mixture to a simmer. Cover the pot with a lid slightly ajar, reduce the heat to low, and let it simmer gently for about 1.5 to 2 hours, or until the beef is tender and can be easily pierced with a fork.
6. Add the carrots and potatoes to the pot. Continue to simmer, partially covered, for another 30-45 minutes, or until the vegetables are tender and the stew has thickened.
7. If using frozen peas, add them to the stew during the last 5 minutes of cooking. Taste and adjust seasoning with salt and pepper if needed.
8. Remove the bay leaves from the stew before serving.
9. Serve the beef stew hot, garnished with chopped fresh parsley if desired.

Enjoy this comforting beef stew with crusty bread or over mashed potatoes for a satisfying meal that the whole family will love!

Macaroni and cheese

Ingredients:

- 8 ounces (about 2 cups) elbow macaroni or any pasta shape you prefer
- 1/4 cup (4 tablespoons) butter
- 1/4 cup all-purpose flour
- 2 cups milk (whole milk for creamier sauce)
- 2 cups shredded cheese (cheddar is traditional, but you can use a mix of cheeses like mozzarella, Gruyère, or Monterey Jack)
- 1/2 teaspoon salt
- 1/4 teaspoon black pepper
- 1/4 teaspoon paprika (optional, for color and flavor)
- 1/4 cup breadcrumbs (optional, for topping)
- Chopped fresh parsley or chives, for garnish (optional)

Instructions:

1. Preheat your oven to 350°F (175°C). Grease a 2-quart baking dish or a 9x13 inch baking pan.
2. Cook the elbow macaroni (or pasta of your choice) according to package instructions until al dente. Drain and set aside.
3. In a large saucepan, melt the butter over medium heat. Add the flour and whisk constantly for about 1 minute to create a roux (a thick paste).
4. Gradually whisk in the milk, ensuring there are no lumps. Cook the mixture, stirring constantly, until it thickens and comes to a simmer, about 5-7 minutes.
5. Reduce the heat to low. Stir in the shredded cheese, a handful at a time, until melted and smooth. Reserve a handful of cheese for topping if desired. Season with salt, black pepper, and paprika.
6. Add the cooked macaroni to the cheese sauce and stir until evenly coated.
7. Pour the macaroni and cheese mixture into the prepared baking dish. Sprinkle the reserved shredded cheese evenly over the top. If using breadcrumbs, sprinkle them evenly over the cheese layer.
8. Bake in the preheated oven for 20-25 minutes, or until the cheese is bubbly and lightly browned on top.
9. Remove from the oven and let it cool for a few minutes before serving.
10. Garnish with chopped fresh parsley or chives if desired, and serve hot.

Enjoy this creamy and cheesy homemade macaroni and cheese as a comforting side dish or main course for the whole family!

Chicken pot pie

Ingredients:

For the filling:

- 2 cups cooked chicken, diced or shredded (you can use leftover roasted chicken or cooked chicken breasts/thighs)
- 1 cup carrots, diced
- 1 cup frozen peas
- 1/2 cup celery, diced
- 1/3 cup butter
- 1/3 cup all-purpose flour
- 1/2 teaspoon salt
- 1/4 teaspoon black pepper
- 1/4 teaspoon dried thyme
- 1/4 teaspoon dried sage
- 1 3/4 cups chicken broth
- 2/3 cup milk (whole milk for creamier sauce)
- Optional: 1/4 cup heavy cream or half-and-half
- Optional: 1 tablespoon chopped fresh parsley

For the crust:

- 1 package (2 sheets) of store-bought puff pastry or pie crust dough, thawed if frozen

Instructions:

1. Preheat your oven to 400°F (200°C). Grease a 9-inch pie dish or a similarly sized baking dish.
2. In a large skillet or saucepan, melt the butter over medium heat. Add the diced carrots, celery, and peas. Cook, stirring occasionally, until the vegetables are slightly tender, about 5-7 minutes.
3. Stir in the flour, salt, pepper, dried thyme, and dried sage. Cook for 1-2 minutes, stirring constantly, to cook off the raw flour taste.
4. Gradually stir in the chicken broth and milk. Bring the mixture to a simmer and cook until thickened, stirring frequently, about 5-7 minutes. If using, add the heavy cream or half-and-half at this stage. The sauce should be thick enough to coat the back of a spoon.
5. Stir in the diced chicken and chopped parsley (if using). Remove the skillet from heat.
6. Roll out one sheet of puff pastry or pie crust dough on a lightly floured surface to fit the size of your baking dish. Place the rolled-out dough into the greased baking dish, pressing it gently against the sides and bottom.
7. Pour the chicken and vegetable filling into the prepared crust.

8. Roll out the second sheet of puff pastry or pie crust dough to fit over the top of the filling. Place the rolled-out dough over the filling, pressing the edges to seal with the bottom crust. Trim any excess dough and crimp the edges with a fork or your fingers to seal.
9. Optional: Cut a few small slits in the top crust to allow steam to escape during baking.
10. Bake in the preheated oven for 30-35 minutes, or until the crust is golden brown and the filling is bubbly.
11. Remove from the oven and let it cool for 5-10 minutes before serving.

Enjoy this comforting and delicious homemade chicken pot pie with your family and friends!

Meatloaf

Ingredients:

- 1.5 pounds (680g) ground beef (you can also use a mix of beef and pork)
- 1 cup breadcrumbs (plain or seasoned)
- 1/2 cup milk
- 1 small onion, finely chopped
- 2 cloves garlic, minced
- 1/4 cup ketchup
- 1/4 cup fresh parsley, chopped (or 1 tablespoon dried parsley)
- 1 tablespoon Worcestershire sauce
- 1 teaspoon salt
- 1/2 teaspoon black pepper
- 1/2 teaspoon dried thyme (optional)
- 2 large eggs, beaten

For the glaze:

- 1/2 cup ketchup
- 2 tablespoons brown sugar
- 1 tablespoon Dijon mustard
- 1 teaspoon Worcestershire sauce

Instructions:

1. Preheat your oven to 350°F (175°C). Grease a 9x5 inch loaf pan or line a baking sheet with parchment paper.
2. In a large mixing bowl, combine the breadcrumbs and milk. Let it sit for a few minutes until the breadcrumbs absorb the milk.
3. Add the ground beef, chopped onion, minced garlic, 1/4 cup ketchup, chopped parsley, Worcestershire sauce, salt, pepper, dried thyme (if using), and beaten eggs to the bowl with the soaked breadcrumbs.
4. Use your hands or a spoon to mix everything together until well combined. Be careful not to overmix, as this can make the meatloaf dense.
5. Transfer the meat mixture to the prepared loaf pan or shape it into a loaf shape on the lined baking sheet.
6. In a small bowl, mix together the ingredients for the glaze: 1/2 cup ketchup, brown sugar, Dijon mustard, and Worcestershire sauce. Spread half of the glaze evenly over the top of the meatloaf.
7. Bake the meatloaf in the preheated oven for 45 minutes.
8. After 45 minutes, remove the meatloaf from the oven and spread the remaining glaze over the top.
9. Return the meatloaf to the oven and bake for an additional 15-20 minutes, or until the internal temperature reaches 160°F (71°C) when tested with a meat thermometer.

10. Remove from the oven and let the meatloaf rest for 10 minutes before slicing.
11. Slice and serve the meatloaf warm, optionally garnished with additional chopped parsley.

Enjoy this classic meatloaf recipe with mashed potatoes, green beans, or your favorite side dishes for a comforting meal!

Tacos

Ingredients:

For the beef filling:

- 1 pound (450g) ground beef
- 1 small onion, finely chopped
- 2 cloves garlic, minced
- 1 tablespoon chili powder
- 1 teaspoon ground cumin
- 1/2 teaspoon paprika
- 1/4 teaspoon dried oregano
- 1/4 teaspoon salt, or to taste
- 1/4 teaspoon black pepper, or to taste
- 1/2 cup tomato sauce
- 1/2 cup beef broth or water

For serving:

- Hard taco shells or soft tortillas
- Shredded lettuce
- Diced tomatoes
- Shredded cheese (such as cheddar or Monterey Jack)
- Sliced jalapeños (optional)
- Sour cream
- Salsa
- Chopped cilantro (optional)
- Lime wedges (for squeezing over tacos)

Instructions:

1. In a large skillet or frying pan, cook the ground beef over medium-high heat until browned and cooked through, breaking it apart with a spatula as it cooks.
2. Add the chopped onion to the skillet with the beef and cook for 2-3 minutes, until the onion is softened.
3. Stir in the minced garlic, chili powder, ground cumin, paprika, dried oregano, salt, and black pepper. Cook for another 1-2 minutes until fragrant.
4. Add the tomato sauce and beef broth (or water) to the skillet, stirring to combine. Bring to a simmer and cook for 5-7 minutes, stirring occasionally, until the sauce has thickened slightly.
5. Taste and adjust seasoning if needed. If the mixture seems too dry, add a little more beef broth or water.

6. While the beef filling is simmering, prepare your taco shells or tortillas according to package instructions. If using hard taco shells, heat them in the oven for a few minutes until crisp.
7. To assemble the tacos, spoon the beef filling into the taco shells or tortillas. Top with shredded lettuce, diced tomatoes, shredded cheese, sliced jalapeños (if using), sour cream, salsa, and chopped cilantro.
8. Serve the tacos immediately, with lime wedges on the side for squeezing over the tacos.

Enjoy these delicious beef tacos with your favorite toppings and sides for a satisfying meal!

Shepherd's pie

Ingredients:

For the mashed potatoes topping:

- 2 pounds (about 1 kg) potatoes, peeled and cut into chunks
- 4 tablespoons butter
- 1/2 cup milk or cream
- Salt and pepper, to taste
- Optional: 1/2 cup shredded cheddar cheese

For the filling:

- 1 tablespoon olive oil
- 1 onion, finely chopped
- 2 cloves garlic, minced
- 1 carrot, diced
- 1 celery stalk, diced
- 1 pound (450g) ground lamb or beef
- 2 tablespoons all-purpose flour
- 1 cup beef broth
- 1 tablespoon tomato paste
- 1 teaspoon Worcestershire sauce
- 1/2 cup frozen peas
- Salt and pepper, to taste
- Optional: chopped fresh herbs like thyme or rosemary

Instructions:

1. Preheat your oven to 375°F (190°C).
2. Place the potatoes in a large pot and cover with water. Bring to a boil over medium-high heat. Cook until the potatoes are fork-tender, about 15-20 minutes.
3. While the potatoes are cooking, heat the olive oil in a large skillet or frying pan over medium heat. Add the chopped onion, garlic, carrot, and celery. Cook, stirring occasionally, until the vegetables are softened, about 5-7 minutes.
4. Add the ground lamb or beef to the skillet. Cook, breaking up the meat with a spatula, until browned and cooked through.
5. Sprinkle the flour over the meat and vegetables in the skillet. Stir to combine and cook for 1-2 minutes.
6. Stir in the beef broth, tomato paste, Worcestershire sauce, and frozen peas. Bring to a simmer and cook for another 5-7 minutes, or until the mixture has thickened slightly. Season with salt, pepper, and optional chopped herbs to taste.

7. While the filling is simmering, drain the cooked potatoes and return them to the pot. Add butter and milk or cream to the pot. Mash the potatoes until smooth and creamy. Season with salt and pepper. Optional: Stir in shredded cheddar cheese for extra richness.
8. Transfer the meat and vegetable filling to a 9x13 inch baking dish or a similarly sized oven-safe dish.
9. Spoon the mashed potatoes over the top of the filling, spreading them evenly with a spatula.
10. Use a fork to create decorative lines or swirls on the surface of the mashed potatoes.
11. Bake in the preheated oven for 25-30 minutes, or until the shepherd's pie is heated through and the mashed potato topping is lightly golden and slightly crispy around the edges.
12. Remove from the oven and let it rest for 5-10 minutes before serving.

Enjoy this comforting shepherd's pie with your family and friends!

Baked ziti

Ingredients:

- 1 pound (450g) ziti pasta (or penne rigate)
- 1 tablespoon olive oil
- 1 onion, finely chopped
- 3 cloves garlic, minced
- 1 pound (450g) Italian sausage (sweet or spicy), casings removed
- 1 can (28 ounces or 800g) crushed tomatoes
- 1 teaspoon dried oregano
- 1 teaspoon dried basil
- Salt and pepper, to taste
- 1/2 teaspoon crushed red pepper flakes (optional, for heat)
- 1 cup ricotta cheese
- 1 cup shredded mozzarella cheese
- 1/2 cup grated Parmesan cheese
- Fresh basil or parsley, chopped (for garnish)

Instructions:

1. Preheat your oven to 375°F (190°C). Grease a 9x13 inch baking dish with olive oil or cooking spray.
2. Cook the ziti pasta in a large pot of salted boiling water according to package instructions until al dente. Drain and set aside.
3. In a large skillet or frying pan, heat the olive oil over medium heat. Add the chopped onion and cook until softened, about 5 minutes. Add the minced garlic and cook for another minute until fragrant.
4. Add the Italian sausage to the skillet, breaking it apart with a spatula. Cook until browned and cooked through, about 8-10 minutes. Drain any excess grease if necessary.
5. Stir in the crushed tomatoes, dried oregano, dried basil, salt, pepper, and crushed red pepper flakes (if using). Bring the sauce to a simmer and cook for 10-15 minutes, stirring occasionally, to allow the flavors to meld. Taste and adjust seasoning if needed.
6. In a large mixing bowl, combine the cooked ziti pasta with the ricotta cheese, shredded mozzarella cheese, and half of the grated Parmesan cheese. Mix until well combined.
7. Spread half of the pasta mixture into the prepared baking dish in an even layer.
8. Spoon half of the sausage and tomato sauce mixture over the pasta layer, spreading it evenly.
9. Repeat with the remaining pasta mixture and sausage sauce mixture.
10. Sprinkle the remaining grated Parmesan cheese evenly over the top.
11. Cover the baking dish with aluminum foil, tenting it slightly to prevent the cheese from sticking.
12. Bake in the preheated oven for 20 minutes. Then, remove the foil and bake for an additional 10-15 minutes, or until the cheese is melted and bubbly and the edges are slightly crispy.

13. Remove from the oven and let it cool for 5-10 minutes before serving.
14. Garnish with chopped fresh basil or parsley before serving.

Enjoy this delicious and comforting baked ziti with garlic bread and a side salad for a complete meal!

Pulled pork sandwiches

Ingredients:

For the pulled pork:

- 3-4 pounds (about 1.5-2 kg) pork shoulder or pork butt
- Salt and pepper
- 2 tablespoons olive oil
- 1 onion, chopped
- 4 cloves garlic, minced
- 1 cup chicken broth or water
- 1 cup barbecue sauce (plus extra for serving)
- 2 tablespoons brown sugar
- 1 tablespoon Worcestershire sauce
- 1 tablespoon apple cider vinegar
- 1 teaspoon smoked paprika
- 1/2 teaspoon cayenne pepper (optional, for heat)

For serving:

- Hamburger buns or sandwich rolls
- Coleslaw (optional, for topping)

Instructions:

1. Season the pork shoulder or pork butt generously with salt and pepper.
2. In a large skillet or frying pan, heat the olive oil over medium-high heat. Sear the pork on all sides until browned, about 3-4 minutes per side. Transfer the seared pork to a slow cooker or a large Dutch oven.
3. In the same skillet or frying pan, add the chopped onion and cook until softened, about 5 minutes. Add the minced garlic and cook for another minute until fragrant.
4. Transfer the cooked onion and garlic to the slow cooker or Dutch oven with the seared pork.
5. In a bowl, mix together the chicken broth or water, barbecue sauce, brown sugar, Worcestershire sauce, apple cider vinegar, smoked paprika, and cayenne pepper (if using). Pour this mixture over the pork in the slow cooker or Dutch oven.
6. If using a slow cooker, cook on low for 8-10 hours or on high for 4-5 hours, until the pork is very tender and easily pulls apart with a fork. If using a Dutch oven, cover and cook in a preheated 325°F (160°C) oven for 3-4 hours, or until the pork is tender.
7. Once the pork is cooked and tender, remove it from the slow cooker or Dutch oven. Use two forks to shred the pork into bite-sized pieces. Remove any excess fat as you shred the meat.
8. Return the shredded pork to the cooking juices in the slow cooker or Dutch oven. Stir to coat the pork with the sauce. Taste and adjust seasoning if needed.

9. To serve, spoon the pulled pork onto hamburger buns or sandwich rolls. Top with extra barbecue sauce and coleslaw if desired.
10. Serve the pulled pork sandwiches hot, accompanied by your favorite sides like potato salad, baked beans, or corn on the cob.

Enjoy these delicious pulled pork sandwiches, packed with flavor and perfect for any occasion!

Chili

Ingredients:

- 1 tablespoon olive oil
- 1 onion, chopped
- 3 cloves garlic, minced
- 1 bell pepper, chopped (any color)
- 1 jalapeño pepper, seeded and finely chopped (optional, for heat)
- 1 pound (450g) ground beef or ground turkey
- 1 can (15 ounces or 400g) kidney beans, drained and rinsed
- 1 can (15 ounces or 400g) black beans, drained and rinsed
- 1 can (15 ounces or 400g) diced tomatoes
- 1 can (6 ounces or 170g) tomato paste
- 2 cups beef broth or chicken broth
- 2 tablespoons chili powder
- 1 tablespoon ground cumin
- 1 teaspoon paprika
- 1/2 teaspoon dried oregano
- 1/2 teaspoon salt, or to taste
- 1/4 teaspoon black pepper, or to taste
- Optional toppings: shredded cheese, sour cream, sliced green onions, chopped cilantro, diced avocado

Instructions:

1. Heat the olive oil in a large pot or Dutch oven over medium heat.
2. Add the chopped onion, garlic, bell pepper, and jalapeño pepper (if using). Cook, stirring occasionally, until the vegetables are softened, about 5-7 minutes.
3. Add the ground beef or ground turkey to the pot. Cook, breaking up the meat with a spatula, until browned and cooked through.
4. Stir in the kidney beans, black beans, diced tomatoes, tomato paste, and beef or chicken broth.
5. Add the chili powder, ground cumin, paprika, dried oregano, salt, and black pepper. Stir to combine well.
6. Bring the chili to a simmer over medium-high heat. Reduce the heat to low and let it simmer, uncovered, stirring occasionally, for 30-45 minutes to allow the flavors to meld and the chili to thicken. If the chili becomes too thick, you can add more broth or water as needed.
7. Taste and adjust seasoning with more salt and pepper if desired.
8. Serve the chili hot, ladled into bowls. Top with shredded cheese, a dollop of sour cream, sliced green onions, chopped cilantro, and diced avocado if desired.
9. Enjoy your homemade chili with cornbread, tortilla chips, or crusty bread on the side.

This recipe makes a generous batch of chili, perfect for feeding a crowd or for leftovers that taste even better the next day! Adjust the spiciness level by adding more or less chili powder and jalapeño according to your preference.

Chicken parmigiana

Ingredients:

For the chicken:

- 4 boneless, skinless chicken breasts
- Salt and pepper
- 1 cup all-purpose flour
- 2 large eggs, beaten
- 1 cup breadcrumbs (Italian seasoned breadcrumbs work well)
- 1/2 cup grated Parmesan cheese
- 1/2 teaspoon garlic powder
- 1/2 teaspoon dried oregano
- 1/2 teaspoon dried basil
- Vegetable oil, for frying

For assembling:

- 2 cups marinara sauce (homemade or store-bought)
- 1 cup shredded mozzarella cheese
- 1/2 cup grated Parmesan cheese
- Fresh basil or parsley, chopped (for garnish)

Instructions:

1. Preheat your oven to 375°F (190°C). Lightly grease a baking dish large enough to fit the chicken breasts in a single layer.
2. Place each chicken breast between two sheets of plastic wrap or parchment paper. Use a meat mallet or rolling pin to pound the chicken to an even thickness, about 1/2 inch thick. This ensures even cooking.
3. Season both sides of each chicken breast with salt and pepper.
4. Set up a breading station: Place the flour in a shallow dish. In another shallow dish, beat the eggs. In a third shallow dish, combine the breadcrumbs, grated Parmesan cheese, garlic powder, dried oregano, and dried basil.
5. Dredge each chicken breast in the flour, shaking off any excess. Dip the chicken into the beaten eggs, allowing any excess to drip off. Press the chicken into the breadcrumb mixture, coating both sides evenly.
6. Heat vegetable oil in a large skillet over medium-high heat. Fry the breaded chicken breasts for about 3-4 minutes per side, or until golden brown and cooked through. Work in batches if needed to avoid overcrowding the skillet. Transfer the cooked chicken to a paper towel-lined plate to drain excess oil.
7. Spread about 1/2 cup of marinara sauce evenly over the bottom of the prepared baking dish. Arrange the fried chicken breasts in a single layer over the sauce.
8. Spoon the remaining marinara sauce over each chicken breast, covering them evenly.

9. Sprinkle shredded mozzarella cheese over each chicken breast, followed by grated Parmesan cheese.
10. Bake in the preheated oven for 20-25 minutes, or until the cheese is melted and bubbly.
11. Remove from the oven and let it rest for a few minutes before serving.
12. Garnish with chopped fresh basil or parsley before serving.

Serve the Chicken Parmigiana hot, alongside pasta, garlic bread, or a fresh green salad for a complete and satisfying meal. Enjoy this classic dish with its crispy exterior, tender chicken, and gooey melted cheese!

Beef stir-fry

Ingredients:

For the beef marinade:

- 1 pound (450g) beef steak (flank steak, sirloin, or any tender cut), thinly sliced against the grain
- 2 tablespoons soy sauce
- 1 tablespoon oyster sauce
- 1 tablespoon cornstarch
- 1 teaspoon sesame oil
- 1/2 teaspoon black pepper

For the stir-fry:

- 2 tablespoons vegetable oil, divided
- 3 cloves garlic, minced
- 1-inch piece of ginger, minced
- 1 onion, thinly sliced
- 1 bell pepper, thinly sliced
- 2 cups broccoli florets
- 1 carrot, thinly sliced
- 1/2 cup snow peas or snap peas
- Optional: sliced mushrooms, baby corn, bamboo shoots, or any other vegetables of your choice

For the sauce:

- 1/4 cup soy sauce
- 2 tablespoons oyster sauce
- 1 tablespoon hoisin sauce (optional)
- 1 tablespoon rice vinegar or white vinegar
- 1 tablespoon brown sugar or honey
- 1/2 cup beef broth or chicken broth
- 1 tablespoon cornstarch mixed with 2 tablespoons water (cornstarch slurry)

Instructions:

1. In a bowl, combine the thinly sliced beef with soy sauce, oyster sauce, cornstarch, sesame oil, and black pepper. Mix well to coat the beef evenly. Let it marinate for at least 15-20 minutes.
2. In a small bowl, mix together the ingredients for the sauce: soy sauce, oyster sauce, hoisin sauce (if using), rice vinegar, brown sugar or honey, and beef or chicken broth.
3. Heat 1 tablespoon of vegetable oil in a large skillet or wok over high heat. Add the marinated beef in a single layer (reserve the marinade) and cook for 2-3 minutes, stirring

occasionally, until browned and cooked through. Remove the beef from the skillet and set aside.
4. Add the remaining 1 tablespoon of vegetable oil to the skillet. Add minced garlic and ginger, and stir-fry for about 30 seconds until fragrant.
5. Add sliced onion, bell pepper, broccoli florets, carrot, snow peas (or snap peas), and any other vegetables you're using. Stir-fry for 3-4 minutes until the vegetables are tender-crisp.
6. Push the vegetables to the sides of the skillet to create a well in the center. Pour in the sauce mixture and bring to a simmer.
7. Stir the cornstarch slurry again to ensure it's well mixed, then pour it into the simmering sauce. Cook for 1-2 minutes, stirring constantly, until the sauce has thickened.
8. Add the cooked beef back into the skillet, along with any juices that have accumulated. Stir everything together to coat the beef and vegetables with the sauce.
9. Cook for another minute or two, until everything is heated through and the sauce coats the beef and vegetables evenly.
10. Remove from heat and serve the beef stir-fry hot, over steamed rice or noodles.

Garnish with sliced green onions and sesame seeds if desired. Enjoy this delicious and satisfying beef stir-fry with your favorite sides for a complete meal!

BBQ ribs

Ingredients:

- 2 racks of pork ribs (baby back ribs or St. Louis style ribs)
- Salt and pepper, to taste
- 1 cup BBQ sauce (homemade or store-bought)

For the dry rub (optional):

- 1/4 cup brown sugar
- 1 tablespoon paprika
- 1 tablespoon garlic powder
- 1 tablespoon onion powder
- 1 tablespoon chili powder
- 1 teaspoon ground cumin
- 1 teaspoon salt
- 1/2 teaspoon black pepper

Instructions:

1. Preheat your oven to 275°F (135°C).
2. Remove the membrane from the back of the ribs, if not already removed. Use a knife to loosen it from one corner of the ribs, then grip it with a paper towel and peel it off.
3. Season the ribs generously with salt and pepper. Optionally, prepare the dry rub by combining all the dry rub ingredients in a bowl. Rub the mixture all over the ribs, coating them evenly. Let the ribs sit at room temperature for about 20-30 minutes to allow the flavors to penetrate.
4. Place the seasoned ribs on a baking sheet lined with aluminum foil, meaty side up. Cover the ribs tightly with another piece of foil, sealing the edges.
5. Bake the ribs in the preheated oven for 2.5 to 3 hours, or until the meat is tender and easily pulls away from the bones. For St. Louis style ribs, which are larger, you may need to bake them for an additional 30 minutes.
6. Remove the ribs from the oven and carefully unwrap them from the foil. Discard the foil and drain any accumulated juices.
7. Preheat your grill to medium-high heat (or prepare a charcoal grill for indirect cooking). Brush the grill grates lightly with oil to prevent sticking.
8. Place the ribs on the grill, meaty side down. Brush the bone side with BBQ sauce and cook for 3-4 minutes, until the sauce caramelizes and forms a crust.
9. Carefully flip the ribs over, so the meaty side is facing up. Brush the top side generously with BBQ sauce and cook for another 3-4 minutes, until the sauce caramelizes and forms a sticky coating.
10. Remove the ribs from the grill and let them rest for a few minutes before slicing them between the bones into individual ribs.
11. Serve the BBQ ribs hot, with extra BBQ sauce on the side for dipping.

Enjoy these delicious BBQ ribs with coleslaw, cornbread, or your favorite sides for a mouthwatering meal!

Fish tacos

Ingredients:

For the fish:

- 1 pound (450g) white fish fillets (such as cod, tilapia, or mahi-mahi)
- 1/2 cup all-purpose flour
- 1 teaspoon ground cumin
- 1 teaspoon chili powder
- 1/2 teaspoon paprika
- 1/2 teaspoon salt
- 1/4 teaspoon black pepper
- Vegetable oil, for frying (about 1/4 cup)

For the slaw:

- 2 cups shredded cabbage (green or purple cabbage, or a mix)
- 1/4 cup chopped fresh cilantro
- 1/4 cup mayonnaise
- 1 tablespoon lime juice
- Salt and pepper, to taste

For assembling:

- 8 small corn or flour tortillas, warmed
- Sliced avocado or guacamole
- Sliced radishes (optional)
- Chopped fresh cilantro, for garnish
- Lime wedges, for serving
- Hot sauce or salsa (optional)

Instructions:

1. Prepare the slaw: In a bowl, combine the shredded cabbage, chopped cilantro, mayonnaise, lime juice, salt, and pepper. Toss until well coated. Adjust seasoning to taste. Set aside.
2. Prepare the fish: Pat the fish fillets dry with paper towels. In a shallow dish, mix together the flour, ground cumin, chili powder, paprika, salt, and pepper.
3. Dredge each fish fillet in the flour mixture, shaking off any excess.
4. Heat vegetable oil in a large skillet over medium-high heat. Add the fish fillets to the skillet and cook for 3-4 minutes per side, or until golden brown and cooked through. The cooking time will depend on the thickness of the fish fillets. Remove the fish from the skillet and place them on a plate lined with paper towels to drain any excess oil.
5. To assemble the tacos, place a few pieces of fried fish on each warm tortilla.
6. Top the fish with a generous spoonful of the prepared slaw.

7. Add sliced avocado or guacamole, sliced radishes (if using), and chopped cilantro on top.
8. Serve the fish tacos immediately with lime wedges on the side for squeezing over the tacos. Offer hot sauce or salsa for those who want an extra kick.

Enjoy these flavorful and fresh fish tacos as a delicious meal for lunch or dinner!

Stuffed peppers

Ingredients:

- 6 large bell peppers (any color), tops cut off and seeds removed
- 1 tablespoon olive oil
- 1 onion, finely chopped
- 3 cloves garlic, minced
- 1 pound (450g) ground beef or turkey
- 1 cup cooked rice (white or brown)
- 1 can (15 ounces or 425g) diced tomatoes, drained
- 1 cup tomato sauce or marinara sauce
- 1 teaspoon dried oregano
- 1 teaspoon dried basil
- Salt and pepper, to taste
- 1 cup shredded mozzarella cheese (or any cheese of your choice)
- Fresh parsley or basil, chopped (for garnish)

Instructions:

1. Preheat your oven to 375°F (190°C). Grease a baking dish large enough to hold all the peppers.
2. Bring a large pot of salted water to a boil. Add the prepared bell peppers and cook for 3-4 minutes, until slightly softened. Remove the peppers from the water and place them upside down on a paper towel to drain excess water.
3. In a large skillet or frying pan, heat olive oil over medium heat. Add the chopped onion and cook until softened, about 5 minutes. Add the minced garlic and cook for another minute until fragrant.
4. Add the ground beef or turkey to the skillet. Cook, breaking up the meat with a spatula, until browned and cooked through.
5. Stir in the cooked rice, drained diced tomatoes, tomato sauce or marinara sauce, dried oregano, dried basil, salt, and pepper. Cook for 5-7 minutes, stirring occasionally, to allow the flavors to meld. Taste and adjust seasoning if needed.
6. Place the prepared bell peppers upright in the greased baking dish.
7. Spoon the meat and rice filling evenly into each bell pepper, packing it down slightly.
8. Cover the baking dish with aluminum foil and bake in the preheated oven for 30 minutes.
9. Remove the foil from the baking dish. Sprinkle shredded mozzarella cheese evenly over each stuffed pepper.
10. Return the baking dish to the oven and bake, uncovered, for an additional 10-15 minutes, or until the cheese is melted and bubbly.
11. Remove from the oven and let the stuffed peppers cool slightly before serving.
12. Garnish with chopped fresh parsley or basil before serving.

Serve these delicious stuffed peppers hot, with a side salad or garlic bread for a satisfying meal!

Shrimp scampi

Ingredients:

- 1 pound (450g) large shrimp, peeled and deveined
- Salt and pepper, to taste
- 3 tablespoons unsalted butter
- 2 tablespoons olive oil
- 4 cloves garlic, minced
- 1/4 teaspoon red pepper flakes (optional, for heat)
- 1/4 cup white wine (such as Pinot Grigio or Sauvignon Blanc)
- 1/4 cup chicken broth or seafood broth
- 1 tablespoon fresh lemon juice
- Zest of 1 lemon
- 1/4 cup chopped fresh parsley
- Cooked pasta or crusty bread, for serving

Instructions:

1. Pat the shrimp dry with paper towels and season with salt and pepper.
2. In a large skillet or frying pan, heat 1 tablespoon of butter and 1 tablespoon of olive oil over medium-high heat.
3. Add the shrimp to the skillet in a single layer (you may need to do this in batches depending on the size of your skillet). Cook the shrimp for 1-2 minutes per side, until pink and opaque. Remove the shrimp from the skillet and set aside.
4. Add the remaining butter and olive oil to the skillet. Add the minced garlic and red pepper flakes (if using). Cook for about 1 minute, stirring constantly, until fragrant.
5. Pour in the white wine and chicken or seafood broth. Bring the mixture to a simmer and cook for 2-3 minutes, allowing the flavors to meld and the liquid to reduce slightly.
6. Stir in the fresh lemon juice and lemon zest.
7. Return the cooked shrimp to the skillet and toss to coat in the sauce. Cook for another 1-2 minutes, until the shrimp are heated through.
8. Remove the skillet from heat and stir in the chopped fresh parsley.
9. Serve the shrimp scampi immediately over cooked pasta or with crusty bread to soak up the delicious sauce.
10. Garnish with additional chopped parsley and lemon wedges if desired.

Enjoy this flavorful shrimp scampi dish as a main course for a special dinner or as a quick and delicious meal any time!

Veggie stir-fry

Ingredients:

- 2 tablespoons vegetable oil (such as canola or sesame oil)
- 1 onion, thinly sliced
- 2 cloves garlic, minced
- 1-inch piece of ginger, minced
- 2 cups broccoli florets
- 1 bell pepper, thinly sliced (any color)
- 1 carrot, julienned or thinly sliced
- 1 zucchini, halved lengthwise and thinly sliced
- 1 cup snap peas or snow peas
- 1 cup mushrooms, sliced (optional)
- 1/2 cup vegetable broth or water
- 2 tablespoons soy sauce (or tamari for gluten-free)
- 1 tablespoon oyster sauce (optional)
- 1 teaspoon sesame oil (optional)
- 1 teaspoon cornstarch mixed with 2 tablespoons water (cornstarch slurry)
- Salt and pepper, to taste
- Cooked rice or noodles, for serving

Instructions:

1. Heat the vegetable oil in a large skillet or wok over medium-high heat.
2. Add the sliced onion and cook for 2-3 minutes until softened.
3. Add the minced garlic and ginger, and cook for another 1 minute until fragrant.
4. Add the broccoli florets, bell pepper, carrot, zucchini, snap peas, and mushrooms (if using). Stir-fry for 4-5 minutes until the vegetables are tender-crisp.
5. In a small bowl, mix together the vegetable broth or water, soy sauce, and oyster sauce (if using). Pour the sauce mixture into the skillet and stir to combine with the vegetables.
6. Cook for 1-2 minutes, allowing the sauce to come to a simmer.
7. Stir in the cornstarch slurry to thicken the sauce. Cook for another minute until the sauce has thickened and coats the vegetables evenly.
8. Taste and adjust seasoning with salt and pepper as needed.
9. Remove the skillet from heat and drizzle with sesame oil (if using) for extra flavor.
10. Serve the veggie stir-fry hot over cooked rice or noodles.

Garnish with chopped green onions, sesame seeds, or fresh cilantro if desired. Enjoy your homemade veggie stir-fry as a delicious and nutritious meal!

Chicken fajitas

Ingredients:

For the marinade:

- 1 pound (450g) boneless, skinless chicken breasts or thighs, sliced into thin strips
- 2 tablespoons olive oil
- Juice of 1 lime
- 2 cloves garlic, minced
- 1 teaspoon chili powder
- 1 teaspoon ground cumin
- 1/2 teaspoon paprika
- 1/2 teaspoon onion powder
- Salt and pepper, to taste

For the fajitas:

- 1 tablespoon vegetable oil
- 1 onion, thinly sliced
- 1 bell pepper, thinly sliced (any color)
- 1 jalapeño pepper, thinly sliced (optional, for heat)
- Salt and pepper, to taste
- 8 small flour tortillas (or corn tortillas for a gluten-free option)
- Optional toppings: shredded cheese, sour cream, guacamole, salsa, chopped cilantro, lime wedges

Instructions:

1. In a bowl, combine the olive oil, lime juice, minced garlic, chili powder, ground cumin, paprika, onion powder, salt, and pepper to make the marinade.
2. Add the sliced chicken strips to the marinade, ensuring they are evenly coated. Cover and refrigerate for at least 30 minutes, or up to 4 hours for maximum flavor.
3. Heat 1 tablespoon of vegetable oil in a large skillet or grill pan over medium-high heat.
4. Add the marinated chicken strips to the skillet in a single layer. Cook for 5-7 minutes, stirring occasionally, until the chicken is cooked through and browned. Remove the chicken from the skillet and set aside.
5. In the same skillet, add a bit more oil if needed. Add the sliced onion, bell pepper, and jalapeño pepper (if using). Season with salt and pepper.
6. Sauté the vegetables for 5-7 minutes, stirring occasionally, until they are tender-crisp and slightly charred.
7. Return the cooked chicken to the skillet with the sautéed vegetables. Stir everything together and cook for another minute or two to heat through.

8. Warm the tortillas: You can heat them in a dry skillet over medium heat for about 30 seconds on each side, or wrap them in foil and warm in a preheated oven at 350°F (175°C) for 5-10 minutes.
9. Serve the chicken fajita mixture hot, spooned into warm tortillas.
10. Serve with optional toppings such as shredded cheese, sour cream, guacamole, salsa, chopped cilantro, and lime wedges on the side.

Enjoy these flavorful chicken fajitas with your favorite toppings for a delicious and satisfying meal!

Beef burritos

Ingredients:

For the beef filling:

- 1 pound (450g) ground beef
- 1 tablespoon olive oil
- 1 onion, finely chopped
- 2 cloves garlic, minced
- 1 bell pepper, finely chopped (any color)
- 1 teaspoon ground cumin
- 1 teaspoon chili powder
- 1/2 teaspoon paprika
- Salt and pepper, to taste
- 1 can (15 ounces or 425g) black beans, drained and rinsed
- 1 cup corn kernels (fresh, frozen, or canned)
- 1/2 cup salsa (store-bought or homemade)

For assembling:

- 8 large flour tortillas (burrito size)
- 2 cups cooked rice (white or brown)
- 1 cup shredded cheese (cheddar, Monterey Jack, or Mexican blend)
- Optional toppings: diced tomatoes, shredded lettuce, sour cream, guacamole, sliced jalapeños, chopped cilantro

Instructions:

1. In a large skillet or frying pan, heat olive oil over medium-high heat. Add the chopped onion and cook for 3-4 minutes until softened.
2. Add the minced garlic and chopped bell pepper to the skillet. Cook for another 2-3 minutes until the bell pepper is tender.
3. Add the ground beef to the skillet. Cook, breaking up the meat with a spatula, until browned and cooked through.
4. Stir in the ground cumin, chili powder, paprika, salt, and pepper. Cook for 1 minute until the spices are fragrant.
5. Add the black beans, corn kernels, and salsa to the skillet. Stir to combine everything well. Cook for another 5 minutes, stirring occasionally, until heated through.
6. Remove the skillet from heat and set aside.
7. Warm the tortillas: You can heat them in a dry skillet over medium heat for about 30 seconds on each side, or wrap them in foil and warm in a preheated oven at 350°F (175°C) for 5-10 minutes.
8. Assemble the burritos: Place a warm tortilla on a clean surface. Spoon a portion of the cooked rice onto the center of the tortilla.

9. Top the rice with a portion of the beef filling mixture.
10. Sprinkle shredded cheese over the beef filling.
11. Fold the sides of the tortilla over the filling, then fold the bottom edge up and over the filling. Roll tightly to enclose the filling completely.
12. Repeat with the remaining tortillas and filling.
13. Serve the beef burritos immediately, with optional toppings such as diced tomatoes, shredded lettuce, sour cream, guacamole, sliced jalapeños, and chopped cilantro.

Enjoy these delicious beef burritos as a complete meal! They are great for a family dinner or for meal prepping lunches for the week.

Ratatouille

Ingredients:

- 1 eggplant, diced
- 2 zucchini, diced
- 1 yellow bell pepper, diced
- 1 red bell pepper, diced
- 1 onion, diced
- 4 cloves garlic, minced
- 2 cups diced tomatoes (fresh or canned)
- 2 tablespoons tomato paste
- 2 tablespoons olive oil
- 1 teaspoon dried thyme (or 2-3 sprigs of fresh thyme)
- 1 teaspoon dried oregano
- Salt and pepper, to taste
- Fresh basil, chopped, for garnish

Instructions:

1. Heat olive oil in a large skillet or Dutch oven over medium heat.
2. Add the diced onion and cook for 3-4 minutes until softened.
3. Add the minced garlic and cook for another minute until fragrant.
4. Add the diced eggplant, zucchini, bell peppers, dried thyme, dried oregano, salt, and pepper. Stir well to combine.
5. Cook the vegetables for 10-12 minutes, stirring occasionally, until they start to soften.
6. Add the diced tomatoes and tomato paste to the skillet. Stir to combine everything well.
7. Reduce the heat to low, cover the skillet, and simmer the ratatouille for 20-25 minutes, stirring occasionally, until all the vegetables are tender and the flavors have melded together.
8. Taste and adjust seasoning with salt and pepper if needed.
9. Remove the skillet from heat and let the ratatouille sit for a few minutes to cool slightly.
10. Serve the ratatouille warm, garnished with chopped fresh basil.

Ratatouille can be served as a main dish, either on its own or with crusty bread, or as a side dish alongside grilled meats or fish. It can also be served cold or at room temperature. Enjoy this rustic and comforting French vegetable stew!

Pad Thai

Ingredients:

- 8 ounces (225g) rice noodles (pad Thai noodles)
- 2 tablespoons tamarind paste
- 3 tablespoons fish sauce
- 2 tablespoons soy sauce
- 1 tablespoon brown sugar (or palm sugar)
- 1/2 teaspoon chili flakes (adjust to taste)
- 2 tablespoons vegetable oil
- 1 shallot, finely chopped
- 2 cloves garlic, minced
- 8 ounces (225g) firm tofu, cut into small cubes (optional)
- 8 ounces (225g) shrimp, peeled and deveined (or chicken, beef, or additional vegetables)
- 2 eggs, lightly beaten
- 1 cup bean sprouts
- 4 green onions, chopped into 1-inch pieces
- 1/4 cup crushed peanuts
- Lime wedges, for serving
- Fresh cilantro, chopped, for garnish

Instructions:

1. Cook the rice noodles according to package instructions until they are just tender. Drain and rinse with cold water to stop cooking. Set aside.
2. In a small bowl, mix together the tamarind paste, fish sauce, soy sauce, brown sugar, and chili flakes. Stir until the sugar is dissolved. This is your Pad Thai sauce.
3. Heat vegetable oil in a large skillet or wok over medium-high heat.
4. Add the chopped shallot and minced garlic. Stir-fry for about 1 minute until fragrant.
5. Add the cubed tofu (if using) to the skillet. Stir-fry for 2-3 minutes until lightly browned.
6. Push the tofu to one side of the skillet and add the shrimp (or other protein) to the empty side. Cook for 2-3 minutes until the shrimp are pink and cooked through.
7. Push the shrimp and tofu to the side and pour the beaten eggs into the empty space in the skillet. Scramble the eggs until they are fully cooked, then mix everything together in the skillet.
8. Add the cooked rice noodles and the Pad Thai sauce to the skillet. Toss everything together gently using tongs or chopsticks, ensuring the noodles are evenly coated with the sauce.
9. Add the bean sprouts and chopped green onions to the skillet. Toss for another minute to heat through.
10. Remove the skillet from heat. Taste and adjust seasoning with more fish sauce, soy sauce, or sugar if needed.

11. Serve Pad Thai hot, garnished with crushed peanuts, lime wedges, and chopped fresh cilantro.

Enjoy this delicious homemade Pad Thai with its authentic Thai flavors and customizable ingredients!

Beef Wellington

Ingredients:

- 1 whole beef tenderloin (about 2 pounds or 900g), trimmed of excess fat
- Salt and pepper, to taste
- 2 tablespoons olive oil
- 3 tablespoons Dijon mustard
- 8-10 slices prosciutto or Parma ham
- 1/2 cup pâté (optional, traditionally foie gras pâté)
- 1 pound (450g) puff pastry, thawed if frozen
- 1 egg, beaten (for egg wash)

For the mushroom duxelles:

- 1 pound (450g) mushrooms (button or cremini), finely chopped
- 2 shallots, finely chopped
- 2 cloves garlic, minced
- 2 tablespoons unsalted butter
- 1 tablespoon olive oil
- Salt and pepper, to taste
- 1/4 cup dry white wine or beef broth
- 1 tablespoon chopped fresh thyme (or 1 teaspoon dried thyme)

Instructions:

1. Season the beef tenderloin generously with salt and pepper.
2. Heat olive oil in a large skillet over high heat. Sear the beef tenderloin on all sides until well-browned, about 2-3 minutes per side. Remove from heat and let it cool slightly.
3. Brush the seared beef tenderloin all over with Dijon mustard.
4. Arrange the slices of prosciutto or Parma ham on a sheet of plastic wrap, slightly overlapping.
5. Spread the pâté (if using) evenly over the ham slices.
6. In the same skillet used for searing the beef, melt butter and olive oil over medium heat. Add chopped shallots and garlic, and cook for 2-3 minutes until softened.
7. Add chopped mushrooms to the skillet, along with salt, pepper, and thyme. Cook, stirring occasionally, until the mushrooms release their moisture and it evaporates, about 10-12 minutes.
8. Add white wine or beef broth to the skillet and cook for another 2-3 minutes until most of the liquid has evaporated. Remove from heat and let the mushroom mixture cool.
9. Roll out the puff pastry on a lightly floured surface to a rectangle large enough to wrap the beef tenderloin.
10. Spread the cooled mushroom mixture evenly over the prosciutto-covered pâté.
11. Place the seared beef tenderloin on top of the mushroom layer.

12. Carefully wrap the puff pastry around the beef tenderloin, sealing the edges and trimming any excess pastry. Brush the pastry with beaten egg to create a golden crust.
13. Transfer the wrapped Beef Wellington onto a baking sheet lined with parchment paper, seam side down.
14. Preheat the oven to 400°F (200°C).
15. Make decorative cuts on top of the pastry with a sharp knife to allow steam to escape during baking.
16. Bake the Beef Wellington in the preheated oven for 40-45 minutes, or until the pastry is golden brown and crispy, and an instant-read thermometer inserted into the center registers 125°F (52°C) for medium-rare or 135°F (57°C) for medium.
17. Remove from the oven and let the Beef Wellington rest for 10-15 minutes before slicing.
18. Serve slices of Beef Wellington with your favorite sides, such as roasted vegetables, mashed potatoes, or a green salad.

Enjoy this elegant and flavorful Beef Wellington as a centerpiece for a special meal!

Chicken tikka masala

Ingredients:

For the chicken marinade:

- 1 pound (450g) boneless, skinless chicken thighs or breasts, cut into bite-sized pieces
- 1/2 cup plain yogurt
- 1 tablespoon lemon juice
- 2 teaspoons ground cumin
- 2 teaspoons ground coriander
- 1 teaspoon paprika
- 1 teaspoon turmeric
- 1 teaspoon garam masala
- 1 teaspoon salt
- 1/2 teaspoon black pepper
- 2 cloves garlic, minced
- 1-inch piece of ginger, grated or minced

For the tikka masala sauce:

- 2 tablespoons vegetable oil or ghee
- 1 onion, finely chopped
- 3 cloves garlic, minced
- 1-inch piece of ginger, grated or minced
- 1 teaspoon ground cumin
- 1 teaspoon ground coriander
- 1 teaspoon paprika
- 1 teaspoon turmeric
- 1/2 teaspoon cayenne pepper (adjust to taste)
- 1 can (15 ounces or 425g) tomato sauce or puree
- 1 cup heavy cream or coconut milk
- 1 teaspoon garam masala
- Salt, to taste
- Fresh cilantro, chopped, for garnish
- Cooked rice or naan, for serving

Instructions:

1. In a bowl, combine all the ingredients for the chicken marinade: yogurt, lemon juice, ground cumin, ground coriander, paprika, turmeric, garam masala, salt, black pepper, minced garlic, and grated ginger. Mix well.
2. Add the chicken pieces to the marinade and toss until evenly coated. Cover and refrigerate for at least 1 hour, or up to overnight for best flavor.

3. Preheat the broiler or grill to medium-high heat. Thread the marinated chicken pieces onto skewers (if using wooden skewers, soak them in water for 30 minutes beforehand to prevent burning).
4. Cook the chicken skewers under the broiler or on the grill for 10-12 minutes, turning halfway through, until the chicken is cooked through and slightly charred. Remove from heat and set aside.
5. In a large skillet or pot, heat vegetable oil or ghee over medium heat. Add the chopped onion and cook for 5-7 minutes until softened and translucent.
6. Add the minced garlic and grated ginger to the skillet. Cook for 1 minute until fragrant.
7. Stir in ground cumin, ground coriander, paprika, turmeric, and cayenne pepper. Cook for another minute to toast the spices.
8. Pour in the tomato sauce or puree. Stir well to combine with the spices and simmer for 5-7 minutes, stirring occasionally.
9. Reduce the heat to low. Stir in the heavy cream or coconut milk and garam masala. Simmer gently for another 5 minutes, stirring occasionally, until the sauce has thickened slightly.
10. Taste the sauce and adjust seasoning with salt as needed.
11. Add the cooked chicken tikka pieces to the sauce. Stir gently to coat the chicken with the sauce.
12. Remove from heat and garnish with chopped fresh cilantro.
13. Serve chicken tikka masala hot over cooked rice or with naan bread on the side.

Enjoy this flavorful and creamy chicken tikka masala with its rich spices and tender chicken pieces, perfect for a satisfying Indian-inspired meal!

Eggplant Parmesan

Ingredients:

- 2 large eggplants, sliced into 1/2-inch rounds
- Salt, for sweating the eggplant
- 1 cup all-purpose flour
- 3 large eggs, beaten
- 2 cups breadcrumbs (preferably Italian-style)
- 1 cup grated Parmesan cheese
- Vegetable oil, for frying
- 2 cups marinara sauce (store-bought or homemade)
- 2 cups shredded mozzarella cheese
- Fresh basil leaves, chopped, for garnish

Instructions:

1. Preheat the oven to 375°F (190°C). Lightly grease a 9x13-inch baking dish with olive oil or cooking spray.
2. Place the eggplant slices in a colander and sprinkle them generously with salt. Let them sit for about 30 minutes to draw out excess moisture. Rinse the eggplant slices under cold water and pat them dry with paper towels.
3. Set up a breading station: Place the flour in one shallow bowl, beaten eggs in another bowl, and combine the breadcrumbs with grated Parmesan cheese in a third bowl.
4. Dip each eggplant slice first in the flour, shaking off any excess, then dip in the beaten eggs, and finally coat evenly with the breadcrumb mixture. Place the breaded eggplant slices on a baking sheet.
5. Heat vegetable oil in a large skillet over medium-high heat. Fry the breaded eggplant slices in batches until golden brown and crispy, about 2-3 minutes per side. Transfer the fried eggplant slices to a paper towel-lined plate to drain excess oil.
6. Spread a thin layer of marinara sauce on the bottom of the prepared baking dish. Arrange a layer of fried eggplant slices over the sauce, overlapping slightly if needed.
7. Spoon more marinara sauce over the eggplant slices, spreading it evenly. Sprinkle shredded mozzarella cheese over the sauce.
8. Repeat the layers of eggplant slices, marinara sauce, and shredded mozzarella cheese until all the ingredients are used, ending with a layer of sauce and cheese on top.
9. Cover the baking dish with aluminum foil and bake in the preheated oven for 30 minutes.
10. Remove the foil and bake for an additional 10-15 minutes, or until the cheese is melted and bubbly, and the edges are golden brown.
11. Remove from the oven and let the Eggplant Parmesan rest for 5-10 minutes before slicing.
12. Garnish with chopped fresh basil leaves before serving.

Serve Eggplant Parmesan hot as a main dish, accompanied by a side salad and garlic bread for a delicious and comforting meal that captures the flavors of Italy. Enjoy!

Beef enchiladas

Ingredients:

For the beef filling:

- 1 pound (450g) lean ground beef
- 1 small onion, finely chopped
- 2 cloves garlic, minced
- 1 teaspoon ground cumin
- 1 teaspoon chili powder
- 1/2 teaspoon paprika
- Salt and pepper, to taste
- 1 can (4 ounces or 113g) diced green chilies, drained (optional)
- 1/4 cup chopped fresh cilantro (optional)

For assembling:

- 10-12 corn tortillas
- 2 cups shredded cheese (cheddar, Monterey Jack, or Mexican blend)
- 2 cups enchilada sauce (store-bought or homemade)

For garnish (optional):

- Chopped fresh cilantro
- Diced avocado
- Sour cream
- Sliced jalapeños
- Sliced green onions

Instructions:

1. Preheat the oven to 375°F (190°C). Lightly grease a 9x13-inch baking dish with cooking spray or olive oil.
2. In a large skillet, cook the ground beef over medium-high heat until browned and cooked through, breaking it up with a spatula as it cooks.
3. Add the chopped onion and minced garlic to the skillet with the ground beef. Cook for 2-3 minutes until the onion is softened and translucent.
4. Stir in the ground cumin, chili powder, paprika, salt, and pepper. Add diced green chilies if using. Cook for another minute until the spices are fragrant.
5. Remove the skillet from heat and stir in chopped fresh cilantro if using. Set aside.
6. Warm the corn tortillas: You can do this by wrapping them in a damp paper towel and microwaving for 30-45 seconds until warm and pliable. Alternatively, you can heat them briefly in a dry skillet over medium heat.
7. Spoon a small amount of enchilada sauce onto the bottom of the prepared baking dish, spreading it evenly.

8. Take a warm tortilla and spoon a generous portion of the beef filling down the center. Sprinkle with shredded cheese.
9. Roll up the tortilla tightly and place it seam-side down in the baking dish. Repeat with the remaining tortillas and filling.
10. Pour the remaining enchilada sauce over the rolled tortillas, spreading it evenly to cover all the tortillas.
11. Sprinkle the remaining shredded cheese over the top of the enchiladas.
12. Cover the baking dish with aluminum foil and bake in the preheated oven for 20-25 minutes, or until the enchiladas are heated through and the cheese is melted and bubbly.
13. Remove the foil and bake for an additional 5 minutes to lightly brown the cheese.
14. Remove from the oven and let the beef enchiladas rest for a few minutes before serving.
15. Garnish with chopped fresh cilantro, diced avocado, sour cream, sliced jalapeños, and sliced green onions if desired.

Serve these delicious beef enchiladas hot as a main dish, accompanied by Mexican rice, refried beans, or a side salad. Enjoy the rich flavors and comforting textures of this classic Mexican dish!

Baked salmon

Ingredients:

- 4 salmon fillets, about 6 ounces (170g) each, skin-on or skinless
- 2 tablespoons olive oil
- 2 cloves garlic, minced
- 1 tablespoon lemon juice
- 1 teaspoon lemon zest
- 1 teaspoon dried oregano (or herb of your choice, such as dill or thyme)
- Salt and pepper, to taste
- Lemon slices, for garnish
- Fresh herbs (parsley, dill, or thyme), chopped, for garnish

Instructions:

1. Preheat the oven to 375°F (190°C). Line a baking sheet with parchment paper or foil for easy cleanup.
2. Place the salmon fillets on the prepared baking sheet, skin-side down if they have skin.
3. In a small bowl, whisk together the olive oil, minced garlic, lemon juice, lemon zest, dried oregano, salt, and pepper.
4. Brush the mixture evenly over the tops of the salmon fillets, coating them well.
5. Place lemon slices on top of each fillet for added flavor and presentation.
6. Bake the salmon in the preheated oven for 12-15 minutes, depending on the thickness of the fillets. The salmon is done when it flakes easily with a fork and reaches an internal temperature of 145°F (63°C).
7. Remove from the oven and let the salmon rest for a few minutes before serving.
8. Garnish with chopped fresh herbs, such as parsley, dill, or thyme.

Serve baked salmon hot, accompanied by your favorite side dishes such as steamed vegetables, rice, or a salad. Baked salmon is versatile and pairs well with many flavors, making it a perfect choice for a healthy and satisfying meal. Enjoy!

Jambalaya

Ingredients:

- 1 pound (450g) boneless, skinless chicken thighs, cut into bite-sized pieces
- 1 pound (450g) andouille sausage, sliced into rounds
- 1 pound (450g) large shrimp, peeled and deveined
- 2 tablespoons olive oil
- 1 onion, finely chopped
- 1 bell pepper (green or red), chopped
- 2 celery stalks, chopped
- 3 cloves garlic, minced
- 1 can (14.5 ounces or 400g) diced tomatoes
- 3 cups chicken broth
- 1 cup long-grain white rice
- 2 teaspoons paprika
- 1 teaspoon dried thyme
- 1 teaspoon dried oregano
- 1/2 teaspoon cayenne pepper (adjust to taste)
- Salt and pepper, to taste
- Fresh parsley, chopped, for garnish

Instructions:

1. Heat olive oil in a large Dutch oven or heavy-bottomed pot over medium-high heat.
2. Add the chicken pieces to the pot and cook until browned on all sides, about 5-7 minutes. Remove the chicken from the pot and set aside.
3. Add the sliced sausage to the pot and cook until browned, about 5 minutes. Remove the sausage from the pot and set aside with the chicken.
4. In the same pot, add chopped onion, bell pepper, and celery. Cook for 5-7 minutes, stirring occasionally, until the vegetables are softened.
5. Add minced garlic to the pot and cook for 1 minute until fragrant.
6. Stir in diced tomatoes (with their juices) and cook for 2-3 minutes.
7. Add chicken broth to the pot and bring to a boil.
8. Stir in rice, paprika, dried thyme, dried oregano, cayenne pepper, salt, and pepper.
9. Return the cooked chicken and sausage to the pot. Reduce heat to low, cover, and simmer for 15-20 minutes, or until the rice is cooked and most of the liquid is absorbed, stirring occasionally.
10. Stir in the shrimp and cook for another 5-7 minutes, or until the shrimp are pink and cooked through.
11. Remove the pot from heat and let the jambalaya sit, covered, for 5 minutes to allow flavors to meld.
12. Taste and adjust seasoning with salt, pepper, and additional cayenne pepper if desired.
13. Garnish jambalaya with chopped fresh parsley before serving.

Serve this hearty and flavorful jambalaya hot, garnished with parsley, alongside crusty bread or cornbread. It's a comforting dish packed with Cajun and Creole flavors that everyone will enjoy!

Swedish meatballs

Ingredients:

For the meatballs:

- 1 pound (450g) ground beef
- 1/2 pound (225g) ground pork (or substitute with more ground beef)
- 1/2 cup breadcrumbs
- 1/4 cup milk
- 1 small onion, finely chopped or grated
- 1 clove garlic, minced
- 1 egg
- 1 teaspoon salt
- 1/2 teaspoon black pepper
- 1/4 teaspoon ground allspice
- 1/4 teaspoon ground nutmeg
- 2 tablespoons chopped fresh parsley (optional)
- 2 tablespoons butter, for frying

For the sauce:

- 3 tablespoons butter
- 3 tablespoons all-purpose flour
- 2 cups beef broth
- 1 cup heavy cream
- 1 tablespoon soy sauce
- Salt and pepper, to taste
- Chopped fresh parsley, for garnish

Instructions:

1. In a small bowl, combine the breadcrumbs and milk. Let it sit for a few minutes until the breadcrumbs absorb the milk.
2. In a large bowl, mix together the ground beef, ground pork, soaked breadcrumbs (squeeze out excess milk), chopped onion, minced garlic, egg, salt, pepper, allspice, nutmeg, and chopped parsley (if using). Mix until well combined.
3. Shape the meat mixture into small meatballs, about 1 inch in diameter.
4. Heat 2 tablespoons of butter in a large skillet over medium-high heat. Add the meatballs in batches and cook until browned on all sides and cooked through, about 8-10 minutes per batch. Transfer cooked meatballs to a plate and set aside.
5. To make the sauce, melt 3 tablespoons of butter in the same skillet over medium heat. Whisk in the flour and cook for 1-2 minutes to make a roux.
6. Gradually whisk in the beef broth, scraping up any browned bits from the bottom of the skillet. Cook, stirring constantly, until the mixture thickens and comes to a simmer.

7. Stir in the heavy cream and soy sauce. Simmer for another 5 minutes, stirring occasionally, until the sauce thickens slightly.
8. Season with salt and pepper to taste.
9. Return the meatballs to the skillet with the sauce. Simmer gently for 5-10 minutes to heat the meatballs through and allow them to absorb some of the sauce.
10. Garnish Swedish meatballs with chopped fresh parsley before serving.

Serve Swedish meatballs hot over mashed potatoes, egg noodles, or with lingonberry sauce on the side for a traditional Swedish accompaniment. Enjoy this comforting and flavorful dish with its creamy sauce and tender meatballs!

Stuffed cabbage rolls

Ingredients:

For the cabbage rolls:

- 1 large head of cabbage
- 1 pound (450g) ground beef (or a mix of beef and pork)
- 1 cup cooked white rice
- 1 onion, finely chopped
- 2 cloves garlic, minced
- 1 egg
- 1 teaspoon salt
- 1/2 teaspoon black pepper
- 1 teaspoon paprika
- 1/2 teaspoon dried thyme
- 1/2 teaspoon dried oregano
- 1/4 teaspoon ground allspice
- 1 can (15 ounces or 425g) tomato sauce or crushed tomatoes

For the sauce:

- 1 can (15 ounces or 425g) tomato sauce or crushed tomatoes
- 1 cup beef broth
- 1 tablespoon brown sugar
- 1 tablespoon apple cider vinegar
- Salt and pepper, to taste

Instructions:

1. Bring a large pot of water to a boil. Carefully remove the core from the cabbage head and place the whole cabbage head in the boiling water. Boil for 3-4 minutes, then carefully remove the outer leaves with tongs as they soften. Repeat until you have about 12 large leaves. Set the leaves aside to cool.
2. In a large bowl, combine ground beef, cooked rice, chopped onion, minced garlic, egg, salt, pepper, paprika, thyme, oregano, and allspice. Mix well until all ingredients are evenly incorporated.
3. Preheat the oven to 350°F (175°C). Prepare a large baking dish by spreading half of the tomato sauce or crushed tomatoes on the bottom.
4. To assemble the cabbage rolls, take one cabbage leaf and place a spoonful of the meat and rice mixture in the center (about 1/3 cup). Fold the sides of the cabbage leaf over the filling, then roll it up tightly to enclose the filling. Place seam-side down in the prepared baking dish. Repeat with remaining cabbage leaves and filling.
5. In a separate bowl, mix together the remaining tomato sauce or crushed tomatoes, beef broth, brown sugar, and apple cider vinegar. Season with salt and pepper to taste.

6. Pour the sauce mixture over the cabbage rolls in the baking dish, covering them evenly.
7. Cover the baking dish tightly with aluminum foil and bake in the preheated oven for 1 hour.
8. After 1 hour, remove the foil and spoon some of the sauce from the bottom of the dish over the cabbage rolls. Bake uncovered for an additional 30 minutes, or until the cabbage rolls are tender and the sauce has thickened slightly.
9. Remove from the oven and let the stuffed cabbage rolls rest for a few minutes before serving.
10. Serve stuffed cabbage rolls hot, spooning extra sauce over each roll. They pair well with mashed potatoes, crusty bread, or a simple green salad.

Enjoy these comforting and flavorful stuffed cabbage rolls, a classic dish that's perfect for a satisfying family meal!

Chicken curry

Ingredients:

- 1.5 pounds (about 700g) boneless, skinless chicken thighs or breasts, cut into bite-sized pieces
- 2 tablespoons vegetable oil or ghee
- 1 large onion, finely chopped
- 3 cloves garlic, minced
- 1 tablespoon ginger, grated or minced
- 2 tablespoons curry powder (adjust to taste)
- 1 teaspoon ground cumin
- 1 teaspoon ground coriander
- 1/2 teaspoon turmeric powder
- 1/4 teaspoon cayenne pepper (adjust to taste)
- 1 can (14 ounces or 400ml) coconut milk
- 1 cup chicken broth
- 2 tablespoons tomato paste
- 2 potatoes, peeled and diced (optional)
- 1 carrot, sliced (optional)
- Salt and pepper, to taste
- Fresh cilantro, chopped, for garnish
- Cooked rice or naan bread, for serving

Instructions:

1. Heat vegetable oil or ghee in a large skillet or pot over medium heat.
2. Add chopped onion and cook until softened and translucent, about 5-7 minutes.
3. Add minced garlic and grated ginger to the skillet. Cook for 1 minute until fragrant.
4. Stir in curry powder, ground cumin, ground coriander, turmeric, and cayenne pepper. Cook for another minute to toast the spices.
5. Add chicken pieces to the skillet and cook until lightly browned on all sides, about 5 minutes.
6. Pour in coconut milk and chicken broth. Stir in tomato paste until well combined.
7. If using potatoes and carrots, add them to the skillet.
8. Bring the mixture to a simmer, then reduce heat to medium-low. Cover and cook for 20-25 minutes, stirring occasionally, until the chicken is cooked through and the vegetables are tender.
9. Taste and adjust seasoning with salt and pepper as needed.
10. Serve chicken curry hot over cooked rice or with naan bread.
11. Garnish with chopped fresh cilantro before serving.

Enjoy this delicious and aromatic chicken curry with its rich, creamy sauce and tender chicken, perfect for a comforting meal with family and friends!

Paella

Ingredients:

- 1 pound (450g) chicken thighs or breasts, cut into bite-sized pieces
- 1/2 pound (225g) Spanish chorizo sausage, sliced
- 1 onion, finely chopped
- 4 cloves garlic, minced
- 1 red bell pepper, thinly sliced
- 1 yellow bell pepper, thinly sliced
- 1 teaspoon smoked paprika
- 1/2 teaspoon saffron threads (optional, but highly recommended)
- 2 cups Arborio rice (or other short-grain rice)
- 1 can (14.5 ounces or 400g) diced tomatoes
- 4 cups chicken broth
- 1 pound (450g) large shrimp, peeled and deveined
- 1/2 pound (225g) mussels, cleaned and debearded (optional)
- Salt and pepper, to taste
- Fresh parsley, chopped, for garnish
- Lemon wedges, for serving

Instructions:

1. Heat olive oil in a large paella pan or skillet over medium-high heat.
2. Add chicken pieces and chorizo sausage slices to the pan. Cook until chicken is browned and chorizo is slightly crisp, about 5-7 minutes. Remove from pan and set aside.
3. In the same pan, add chopped onion and cook for 3-4 minutes until softened.
4. Add minced garlic, sliced bell peppers, smoked paprika, and saffron threads (if using). Cook for another 2 minutes until fragrant.
5. Stir in Arborio rice and cook for 1-2 minutes, stirring constantly, until rice is well coated with oil and slightly toasted.
6. Pour in diced tomatoes (with their juices) and chicken broth. Stir to combine.
7. Bring the mixture to a boil, then reduce heat to medium-low. Simmer uncovered for 15-20 minutes, stirring occasionally, until most of the liquid is absorbed and the rice is nearly tender.
8. Nestle the cooked chicken and chorizo back into the rice mixture.
9. Arrange shrimp and mussels (if using) over the rice. Cover with a lid or aluminum foil and cook for 5-7 minutes, or until the shrimp are pink and opaque, and the mussels have opened.
10. Remove from heat and let the paella rest, covered, for 5 minutes.
11. Season with salt and pepper to taste. Garnish with chopped fresh parsley and serve with lemon wedges on the side.

Paella is traditionally served directly from the pan, so bring it to the table and let everyone dig in! Enjoy this flavorful and colorful Spanish dish, perfect for sharing with family and friends.

Beef kebabs

Ingredients:

- 1.5 pounds (about 700g) beef sirloin or tenderloin, cut into 1-inch cubes
- 1 onion, cut into chunks
- 1 bell pepper (any color), cut into chunks
- 8-10 cherry tomatoes
- Wooden or metal skewers (if using wooden skewers, soak them in water for 30 minutes before using)

For the marinade:

- 1/4 cup soy sauce
- 1/4 cup olive oil
- 2 tablespoons Worcestershire sauce
- 2 cloves garlic, minced
- 1 teaspoon dried oregano
- 1 teaspoon dried thyme
- 1/2 teaspoon black pepper
- 1/2 teaspoon paprika
- 1/4 teaspoon cayenne pepper (optional, for heat)

Instructions:

1. In a bowl, whisk together all the ingredients for the marinade: soy sauce, olive oil, Worcestershire sauce, minced garlic, dried oregano, dried thyme, black pepper, paprika, and cayenne pepper (if using).
2. Place the beef cubes in a large resealable plastic bag or shallow dish. Pour the marinade over the beef, making sure it is well coated. Seal the bag or cover the dish and refrigerate for at least 1 hour, or overnight for best flavor.
3. If using wooden skewers, soak them in water for at least 30 minutes to prevent them from burning.
4. Preheat the grill to medium-high heat.
5. Thread the marinated beef cubes onto the skewers, alternating with chunks of onion, bell pepper, and cherry tomatoes.
6. Brush the grill grates lightly with oil to prevent sticking. Place the beef skewers on the grill and cook for 10-12 minutes, turning occasionally, until the beef is cooked to your desired doneness and the vegetables are tender and slightly charred.
7. Remove the beef skewers from the grill and let them rest for a few minutes before serving.
8. Serve beef kebabs hot, garnished with fresh herbs like parsley or cilantro if desired. They pair well with rice, couscous, or a fresh salad.

Enjoy these tender and flavorful beef kebabs, perfect for a summer barbecue or any time you want a delicious and satisfying meal!

Egg fried rice

Ingredients:

- 3 cups cooked rice (preferably day-old and cooled)
- 2 tablespoons vegetable oil
- 2 eggs, lightly beaten
- 1 onion, finely chopped
- 2 cloves garlic, minced
- 1 cup mixed vegetables (such as peas, carrots, and corn)
- 2-3 tablespoons soy sauce (adjust to taste)
- 1 teaspoon sesame oil (optional)
- Salt and pepper, to taste
- Green onions, chopped, for garnish (optional)

Instructions:

1. Heat vegetable oil in a large skillet or wok over medium heat.
2. Add beaten eggs to the skillet and cook, stirring gently, until scrambled and just set. Remove the scrambled eggs from the skillet and set aside.
3. In the same skillet, add chopped onion and cook for 2-3 minutes until softened.
4. Add minced garlic and mixed vegetables to the skillet. Cook for another 3-4 minutes, stirring frequently, until vegetables are tender.
5. Increase the heat to medium-high. Add cooked rice to the skillet, breaking up any clumps with a spoon or spatula.
6. Drizzle soy sauce and sesame oil (if using) over the rice. Stir well to combine and evenly distribute the soy sauce throughout the rice. Cook for 3-4 minutes, stirring frequently, until the rice is heated through.
7. Return the scrambled eggs to the skillet with the rice and vegetables. Stir gently to combine and heat through.
8. Taste and adjust seasoning with salt, pepper, and more soy sauce if needed.
9. Remove from heat and garnish with chopped green onions, if desired.

Serve egg fried rice hot as a main dish or as a side with your favorite Asian dishes such as stir-fries or grilled meats. Enjoy the delicious flavors and comforting textures of homemade egg fried rice!

Chicken noodle soup

Ingredients:

- 1 tablespoon olive oil
- 1 onion, chopped
- 2 carrots, sliced
- 2 celery stalks, sliced
- 2 cloves garlic, minced
- 1 teaspoon dried thyme
- 1 bay leaf
- 8 cups chicken broth (homemade or store-bought)
- 2 cups cooked chicken breast, shredded or chopped
- 2 cups egg noodles (or any pasta of your choice)
- Salt and pepper, to taste
- Fresh parsley, chopped, for garnish (optional)
- Lemon wedges, for serving (optional)

Instructions:

1. In a large pot or Dutch oven, heat olive oil over medium heat.
2. Add chopped onion, sliced carrots, and sliced celery to the pot. Cook for 5-7 minutes, stirring occasionally, until vegetables are softened.
3. Add minced garlic, dried thyme, and bay leaf to the pot. Cook for 1 minute until fragrant.
4. Pour in chicken broth and bring to a boil.
5. Once boiling, reduce heat to medium-low and simmer for 10 minutes, allowing the flavors to meld.
6. Add cooked chicken breast and egg noodles to the pot. Cook for 8-10 minutes, or until noodles are tender and cooked through.
7. Season with salt and pepper to taste.
8. Remove bay leaf from the soup.
9. Serve hot, garnished with chopped fresh parsley and accompanied by lemon wedges if desired.

Enjoy this comforting chicken noodle soup on its own or with a side of crusty bread. It's a classic dish that warms both the body and soul!

Goulash

Ingredients:

- 2 tablespoons vegetable oil
- 1 large onion, chopped
- 2 cloves garlic, minced
- 2 pounds (about 900g) beef stew meat, cut into bite-sized pieces
- 2 tablespoons sweet paprika
- 1 teaspoon smoked paprika (optional, for additional smokiness)
- 1 teaspoon caraway seeds (optional)
- Salt and pepper, to taste
- 2 tablespoons tomato paste
- 4 cups beef broth
- 1 large potato, peeled and diced
- 2 carrots, sliced
- 1 bell pepper (any color), diced
- 1 cup diced tomatoes (canned or fresh)
- 1/2 cup sour cream (optional, for serving)
- Chopped fresh parsley or dill, for garnish

Instructions:

1. Heat vegetable oil in a large Dutch oven or heavy-bottomed pot over medium heat.
2. Add chopped onion and cook for 5-7 minutes, until softened.
3. Add minced garlic and cook for 1 minute until fragrant.
4. Add beef stew meat to the pot, season with salt and pepper, and cook until browned on all sides, about 5-7 minutes.
5. Stir in sweet paprika, smoked paprika (if using), and caraway seeds (if using). Cook for 1 minute to toast the spices.
6. Add tomato paste to the pot and stir to coat the meat and onions.
7. Pour in beef broth and bring to a boil.
8. Reduce heat to low, cover, and simmer for 1.5 to 2 hours, stirring occasionally, until the beef is tender.
9. Add diced potato, sliced carrots, diced bell pepper, and diced tomatoes to the pot. Stir to combine.
10. Cover and continue to simmer for another 30-40 minutes, or until the vegetables are tender and the sauce has thickened.
11. Taste and adjust seasoning with salt and pepper if needed.
12. Remove from heat and let the goulash rest for a few minutes before serving.
13. Serve hot, garnished with a dollop of sour cream (if using) and chopped fresh parsley or dill.

Goulash is traditionally served with bread, dumplings, or over mashed potatoes. Enjoy this comforting and flavorful dish that's perfect for colder weather!

Stuffed mushrooms

Ingredients:

- 12 large mushrooms (cremini or button mushrooms work well)
- 1 tablespoon olive oil
- 2 cloves garlic, minced
- 1/2 onion, finely chopped
- 1/4 cup breadcrumbs
- 1/4 cup grated Parmesan cheese
- 2 tablespoons chopped fresh parsley
- Salt and pepper, to taste
- 2 tablespoons butter, melted

Instructions:

1. Preheat the oven to 375°F (190°C). Line a baking sheet with parchment paper or foil.
2. Clean the mushrooms with a damp cloth or paper towel to remove any dirt. Remove the stems from the mushrooms and finely chop them.
3. Heat olive oil in a skillet over medium heat. Add minced garlic and chopped onion, and cook until softened, about 3-4 minutes.
4. Add chopped mushroom stems to the skillet and cook for another 3-4 minutes until they release their moisture and are tender.
5. Remove the skillet from heat and stir in breadcrumbs, grated Parmesan cheese, chopped parsley, salt, and pepper. Mix well to combine.
6. Spoon the filling mixture into the mushroom caps, pressing gently to pack the filling.
7. Place the stuffed mushrooms on the prepared baking sheet. Drizzle melted butter over the stuffed mushrooms.
8. Bake in the preheated oven for 20-25 minutes, or until the mushrooms are tender and the filling is golden brown on top.
9. Remove from the oven and let the stuffed mushrooms cool slightly before serving.
10. Garnish with additional chopped parsley if desired.

Enjoy these savory stuffed mushrooms as a delicious appetizer or side dish for any occasion!

Lemon garlic butter shrimp

Ingredients:

- 1 pound (450g) large shrimp, peeled and deveined
- 4 tablespoons unsalted butter
- 4 cloves garlic, minced
- Zest of 1 lemon
- Juice of 1 lemon
- 1/4 teaspoon red pepper flakes (optional, for heat)
- Salt and pepper, to taste
- 2 tablespoons chopped fresh parsley

Instructions:

1. Pat the shrimp dry with paper towels and season with salt and pepper.
2. In a large skillet, melt 2 tablespoons of butter over medium-high heat.
3. Add minced garlic to the skillet and cook for 1 minute until fragrant.
4. Add the shrimp to the skillet in a single layer. Cook for 2-3 minutes per side, until shrimp are pink and opaque. Remove shrimp from skillet and set aside.
5. In the same skillet, add the remaining 2 tablespoons of butter. Allow it to melt and start to bubble.
6. Stir in lemon zest, lemon juice, and red pepper flakes (if using). Cook for 1-2 minutes, stirring constantly, until the sauce thickens slightly.
7. Return the cooked shrimp to the skillet and toss to coat evenly with the lemon garlic butter sauce.
8. Remove from heat and garnish with chopped fresh parsley.
9. Serve immediately, preferably over rice, pasta, or with crusty bread to soak up the delicious sauce.

Enjoy this flavorful and aromatic lemon garlic butter shrimp as a main dish. It's bursting with citrusy flavors and pairs wonderfully with a variety of side dishes!

Baked potato soup

Ingredients:

- 4 large russet potatoes (about 2 pounds), scrubbed clean
- 4 tablespoons unsalted butter
- 1 onion, finely chopped
- 4 cloves garlic, minced
- 1/4 cup all-purpose flour
- 4 cups chicken broth (or vegetable broth for a vegetarian option)
- 2 cups milk (whole milk or 2%)
- 1 cup sour cream
- 1 cup shredded cheddar cheese, plus more for garnish
- Salt and pepper, to taste
- Optional toppings: chopped green onions, crispy bacon bits, additional shredded cheese, sour cream

Instructions:

1. Preheat the oven to 400°F (200°C). Place the scrubbed potatoes on a baking sheet and pierce them with a fork a few times. Bake for 45-60 minutes, or until the potatoes are tender when pierced with a fork. Remove from the oven and let them cool slightly.
2. While the potatoes are baking, melt butter in a large pot or Dutch oven over medium heat.
3. Add chopped onion to the pot and cook for 5-7 minutes, until softened and translucent.
4. Add minced garlic to the pot and cook for 1 minute until fragrant.
5. Sprinkle flour over the onion and garlic mixture. Stir well to combine and cook for 1-2 minutes to cook out the raw flour taste.
6. Gradually pour in chicken broth, stirring constantly to prevent lumps. Bring to a simmer and cook for 5-7 minutes, until slightly thickened.
7. Meanwhile, peel the baked potatoes (if desired) and roughly chop them into bite-sized pieces.
8. Add chopped potatoes and milk to the pot. Stir well to combine and bring back to a simmer.
9. Reduce heat to low. Stir in sour cream and shredded cheddar cheese until melted and smooth. Season with salt and pepper to taste.
10. Simmer gently for another 5-10 minutes to allow the flavors to meld together, stirring occasionally.
11. Serve hot, garnished with additional shredded cheese, chopped green onions, crispy bacon bits, and a dollop of sour cream if desired.

Enjoy this creamy and comforting baked potato soup as a main dish or a starter. It's sure to warm you up from the inside out!

Pork schnitzel

Ingredients:

- 4 boneless pork chops, about 1/2 inch thick (you can also use pork tenderloin and slice it into thin cutlets)
- Salt and pepper, to taste
- 1/2 cup all-purpose flour
- 2 large eggs
- 1 cup breadcrumbs (preferably fresh breadcrumbs for best texture)
- 1/2 teaspoon paprika
- Vegetable oil or clarified butter, for frying
- Lemon wedges, for serving

Instructions:

1. Place each pork chop between two sheets of plastic wrap or parchment paper. Use a meat mallet or the bottom of a heavy skillet to pound the pork chops until they are about 1/4 inch thick. Season both sides of each pork cutlet with salt and pepper.
2. Set up a breading station: Place flour on a shallow plate. In a shallow bowl, beat the eggs. In another shallow plate, mix breadcrumbs with paprika.
3. Dredge each pork cutlet in the flour, shaking off any excess. Dip into the beaten eggs, allowing excess to drip off. Finally, coat evenly with the breadcrumb mixture, pressing gently to adhere.
4. Heat vegetable oil or clarified butter in a large skillet over medium-high heat. Add enough oil to cover the bottom of the skillet about 1/4 inch deep.
5. Once the oil is hot (about 350°F or 175°C), carefully add the breaded pork cutlets to the skillet in batches (do not overcrowd the pan). Fry for 3-4 minutes on each side, or until the schnitzels are golden brown and cooked through. The internal temperature of the pork should reach 145°F (63°C).
6. Remove the schnitzels from the skillet and transfer to a paper towel-lined plate to drain excess oil. Keep warm while you fry the remaining schnitzels.
7. Serve hot, garnished with lemon wedges for squeezing over the schnitzels.

Pork schnitzel is traditionally served with sides like German potato salad, mashed potatoes, or cucumber salad. Enjoy this crispy and delicious dish with its tender pork and crunchy breadcrumb coating!

Teriyaki chicken

Ingredients:

- 4 boneless, skinless chicken thighs (or chicken breasts), cut into bite-sized pieces
- 1/4 cup soy sauce (low sodium recommended)
- 1/4 cup mirin (Japanese sweet rice wine)
- 2 tablespoons sake (Japanese rice wine) or dry white wine
- 2 tablespoons brown sugar (or granulated sugar)
- 1 clove garlic, minced
- 1 teaspoon grated fresh ginger
- 1 tablespoon cornstarch (optional, for thickening the sauce)
- 1 tablespoon water (optional, for cornstarch slurry)
- Vegetable oil, for cooking
- Sesame seeds and chopped green onions, for garnish

Instructions:

1. In a bowl, whisk together soy sauce, mirin, sake (or white wine), brown sugar, minced garlic, and grated ginger until the sugar is dissolved.
2. Place the chicken pieces in a shallow dish or resealable plastic bag. Pour half of the teriyaki sauce over the chicken, reserving the other half for later. Marinate the chicken for at least 30 minutes in the refrigerator, or up to 2 hours for more flavor.
3. Heat a tablespoon of vegetable oil in a large skillet or wok over medium-high heat.
4. Remove the chicken from the marinade (discard the marinade) and add it to the hot skillet. Cook the chicken, stirring occasionally, until it is cooked through and lightly browned, about 6-8 minutes.
5. While the chicken is cooking, you can prepare the optional cornstarch slurry: In a small bowl, mix together cornstarch and water until smooth.
6. When the chicken is cooked through, reduce the heat to medium-low and add the reserved teriyaki sauce to the skillet. If using, stir in the cornstarch slurry to thicken the sauce. Cook for an additional 1-2 minutes, stirring constantly, until the sauce has thickened slightly and coats the chicken.
7. Remove from heat and garnish with sesame seeds and chopped green onions.
8. Serve hot teriyaki chicken over steamed rice and with your favorite steamed vegetables.

Enjoy this homemade teriyaki chicken with its delicious sweet and savory flavors! It's a comforting and satisfying dish that's easy to make at home.

Spanakopita

Ingredients:

- 1 pound (450g) fresh spinach, washed and trimmed (you can also use frozen spinach, thawed and drained)
- 1 bunch green onions, finely chopped
- 1/2 cup fresh dill, chopped (or 2 tablespoons dried dill)
- 1/2 cup fresh parsley, chopped
- 8 ounces (about 225g) feta cheese, crumbled
- 4 ounces (about 115g) ricotta cheese (optional, for a creamier filling)
- 2 eggs, lightly beaten
- Salt and pepper, to taste
- 1/4 teaspoon ground nutmeg
- 1/2 cup (1 stick) unsalted butter, melted
- 1/2 pound (about 225g) phyllo dough, thawed if frozen

Instructions:

1. Preheat the oven to 350°F (175°C). Lightly grease a 9x13-inch baking dish with butter or cooking spray.
2. If using fresh spinach, blanch it in boiling water for 1-2 minutes until wilted. Drain well, squeeze out excess moisture, and chop finely. If using frozen spinach, thaw and drain well.
3. In a large bowl, combine chopped spinach, green onions, dill, parsley, feta cheese, ricotta cheese (if using), and beaten eggs. Season with salt, pepper, and nutmeg. Mix well to combine.
4. Unroll the phyllo dough sheets and cover with a damp towel to prevent them from drying out.
5. Place one sheet of phyllo dough in the prepared baking dish and brush lightly with melted butter. Repeat with 7 more sheets, brushing each layer with butter.
6. Spread half of the spinach and cheese mixture evenly over the phyllo dough in the dish.
7. Top with 8 more sheets of phyllo dough, brushing each layer with melted butter.
8. Spread the remaining spinach and cheese mixture over the phyllo dough.
9. Layer the remaining phyllo dough sheets on top, brushing each sheet with melted butter. Brush the top layer generously with butter.
10. Using a sharp knife, carefully score the top layer of phyllo into squares or diamonds, being careful not to cut all the way through to the bottom.
11. Bake in the preheated oven for 45-50 minutes, or until the spanakopita is golden brown and crisp.
12. Remove from the oven and let it cool slightly before slicing and serving.

Spanakopita is delicious served warm or at room temperature. It makes a wonderful appetizer, side dish, or even a light meal when paired with a salad. Enjoy the flavors of Greece with this classic spanakopita recipe!

Cornbread

Ingredients:

- 1 cup cornmeal
- 1 cup all-purpose flour
- 1/4 cup granulated sugar (optional, adjust to taste)
- 1 tablespoon baking powder
- 1/2 teaspoon baking soda
- 1/2 teaspoon salt
- 1 cup buttermilk (or 1 cup milk + 1 tablespoon vinegar or lemon juice, let sit for 5 minutes)
- 1/2 cup unsalted butter, melted and cooled slightly
- 2 large eggs, lightly beaten
- 1/4 cup honey (optional, for added sweetness)

Instructions:

1. Preheat your oven to 400°F (200°C). Grease a 9-inch square baking pan or a 9-inch cast iron skillet.
2. In a large bowl, whisk together the cornmeal, flour, sugar (if using), baking powder, baking soda, and salt.
3. In another bowl, whisk together the buttermilk, melted butter, eggs, and honey (if using).
4. Pour the wet ingredients into the dry ingredients and stir until just combined. Do not overmix; a few lumps are okay.
5. Pour the batter into the prepared baking pan or skillet, spreading it out evenly.
6. Bake for 20-25 minutes, or until the cornbread is golden brown and a toothpick inserted into the center comes out clean.
7. Remove from the oven and let it cool in the pan for 10 minutes before slicing and serving.
8. Serve warm with butter and honey, or alongside chili, soups, stews, or barbecue dishes.

Enjoy this homemade cornbread with its moist texture and slightly sweet flavor. It's perfect for any meal or occasion, bringing a taste of Southern comfort to your table!

Quiche Lorraine

Ingredients:

For the pastry crust:

- 1 1/4 cups all-purpose flour
- 1/2 teaspoon salt
- 1/2 cup (1 stick) unsalted butter, chilled and cut into small pieces
- 3-4 tablespoons ice water

For the filling:

- 8 ounces (about 225g) bacon or lardons, chopped
- 1 cup grated Gruyère cheese (or Swiss cheese)
- 4 large eggs
- 1 cup heavy cream (or half-and-half)
- Salt and pepper, to taste
- Pinch of nutmeg (optional)

Instructions:

1. To make the pastry crust, combine the flour and salt in a large bowl. Add the chilled butter pieces and use a pastry cutter or your fingers to cut the butter into the flour until the mixture resembles coarse crumbs.
2. Gradually add the ice water, 1 tablespoon at a time, mixing with a fork until the dough just holds together when pressed. Be careful not to overwork the dough.
3. Shape the dough into a disk, wrap it in plastic wrap, and refrigerate for at least 1 hour (or up to overnight).
4. Preheat your oven to 375°F (190°C). On a lightly floured surface, roll out the chilled dough into a circle about 12 inches in diameter. Carefully transfer the dough to a 9-inch tart pan or pie dish. Press the dough into the bottom and up the sides of the pan. Trim any excess dough and prick the bottom of the crust with a fork.
5. Line the crust with parchment paper or aluminum foil and fill with pie weights or dried beans. Bake for 15 minutes. Remove the parchment paper and weights/beans, then bake for an additional 5 minutes until the crust is lightly golden. Remove from the oven and let it cool slightly while preparing the filling.
6. In a skillet, cook the chopped bacon or lardons over medium heat until crisp. Remove from the skillet and drain on paper towels.
7. Sprinkle the grated cheese and cooked bacon evenly over the bottom of the pre-baked pastry crust.
8. In a bowl, whisk together the eggs, heavy cream (or half-and-half), salt, pepper, and nutmeg (if using) until well combined.
9. Pour the egg mixture over the cheese and bacon in the crust, filling it almost to the top.

10. Bake the quiche in the preheated oven for 30-35 minutes, or until the filling is set and the top is golden brown.
11. Remove from the oven and let it cool slightly before slicing and serving.

Quiche Lorraine can be served warm or at room temperature, making it a versatile dish for brunch, lunch, or even a light dinner. Enjoy the creamy custard filling with its savory bacon and cheese flavors, all nestled in a flaky pastry crust!

Beef pot pie

Ingredients:

For the filling:

- 1 pound (450g) beef stew meat, cut into bite-sized pieces
- Salt and pepper, to taste
- 2 tablespoons vegetable oil
- 1 onion, chopped
- 2 cloves garlic, minced
- 2 carrots, peeled and diced
- 2 celery stalks, diced
- 1 cup frozen peas
- 1 teaspoon dried thyme
- 1/2 teaspoon dried rosemary
- 1/4 cup all-purpose flour
- 2 cups beef broth
- 1/2 cup heavy cream (optional, for a richer filling)

For the pastry crust:

- 1 sheet store-bought puff pastry or pie crust, thawed if frozen

Instructions:

1. Preheat your oven to 375°F (190°C).
2. Season the beef stew meat with salt and pepper. In a large skillet or Dutch oven, heat the vegetable oil over medium-high heat. Add the beef in batches and cook until browned on all sides. Remove the beef from the skillet and set aside.
3. In the same skillet, add chopped onion, minced garlic, diced carrots, and diced celery. Cook for 5-7 minutes, until the vegetables are softened.
4. Add the frozen peas, dried thyme, and dried rosemary to the skillet. Cook for another 2 minutes.
5. Sprinkle flour over the vegetables and stir to coat evenly. Cook for 1-2 minutes to cook out the raw flour taste.
6. Gradually pour in the beef broth, stirring constantly to prevent lumps. Bring to a simmer and cook for 5-7 minutes, until the sauce has thickened.
7. If using, stir in the heavy cream for a richer filling. Add the browned beef back to the skillet and stir to combine. Remove from heat.
8. Transfer the beef filling to a 9-inch pie dish or any oven-safe baking dish.
9. Roll out the puff pastry or pie crust on a lightly floured surface to fit the size of your baking dish. Place the pastry over the filling, pressing gently to adhere to the edges of the dish. Trim any excess pastry and crimp the edges with a fork.
10. Cut a few slits in the top of the pastry to allow steam to escape during baking.

11. Bake in the preheated oven for 30-35 minutes, or until the pastry is golden brown and the filling is bubbling.
12. Remove from the oven and let it cool for a few minutes before serving.

Beef pot pie is best served warm, allowing the flavors to meld together. It's a comforting dish perfect for a cozy dinner or a gathering with family and friends. Enjoy the tender beef, savory vegetables, and flaky pastry crust!

Ceviche

Ingredients:

- 1 pound (450g) firm white fish fillets (such as sea bass, snapper, or halibut), cut into bite-sized pieces
- 1 cup freshly squeezed lime juice (about 8-10 limes)
- 1/2 red onion, thinly sliced
- 1-2 fresh hot peppers (such as jalapeño or serrano), seeded and finely chopped (adjust to taste)
- 1/2 cup chopped fresh cilantro leaves
- 1-2 tomatoes, seeded and diced
- 1 avocado, diced (optional)
- Salt and pepper, to taste
- Corn tortilla chips or lettuce leaves, for serving

Instructions:

1. In a glass or non-reactive bowl, combine the fish pieces and freshly squeezed lime juice. Make sure the fish is completely submerged in the lime juice. Cover the bowl and refrigerate for at least 30 minutes to 1 hour, or until the fish is opaque and "cooked" through (the flesh should turn from translucent to opaque).
2. While the fish is marinating, prepare the other ingredients: thinly slice the red onion, chop the hot peppers, dice the tomatoes, and chop the cilantro leaves.
3. Drain the lime juice from the fish. Discard the lime juice or reserve a small amount for adjusting the seasoning later.
4. Add the sliced red onion, chopped hot peppers, diced tomatoes, and chopped cilantro to the fish. Gently toss to combine.
5. Season the ceviche with salt and pepper to taste. If desired, gently fold in diced avocado.
6. Serve the ceviche immediately, garnished with additional cilantro leaves and accompanied by corn tortilla chips or lettuce leaves for scooping.
7. Enjoy the ceviche as a refreshing appetizer or light main dish.

Note: Ceviche is best served fresh shortly after preparing, as the texture of the fish may change if left for too long in the acidic marinade. Adjust the amount of hot peppers according to your spice preference.

This traditional ceviche recipe highlights the fresh flavors of the seafood and citrus, complemented by the crispness of the vegetables and herbs. It's a perfect dish for warm weather or any occasion where you want to enjoy a light and flavorful seafood dish.

Chicken and dumplings

Ingredients:

For the chicken:

- 1 whole chicken (about 3-4 pounds), cut into pieces (or 4-6 bone-in, skin-on chicken thighs or breasts)
- Salt and pepper, to taste
- 2 tablespoons vegetable oil
- 1 onion, chopped
- 2 carrots, peeled and sliced
- 2 celery stalks, sliced
- 4 cloves garlic, minced
- 6 cups chicken broth
- 1 bay leaf
- 1 teaspoon dried thyme
- 1 teaspoon dried parsley
- 1/2 teaspoon dried rosemary
- 1/2 teaspoon dried sage (optional)
- 1 cup frozen peas (optional)
- 1/2 cup heavy cream (optional, for a richer broth)

For the dumplings:

- 2 cups all-purpose flour
- 1 tablespoon baking powder
- 1 teaspoon salt
- 1/2 teaspoon black pepper
- 1/4 cup unsalted butter, cold and cut into small pieces
- 3/4 cup milk

Instructions:

1. Season the chicken pieces with salt and pepper.
2. In a large pot or Dutch oven, heat vegetable oil over medium-high heat. Add the chicken pieces and cook until browned on all sides, about 5-7 minutes per side. Remove the chicken from the pot and set aside.
3. Add chopped onion, sliced carrots, and sliced celery to the pot. Cook for 5-7 minutes, until vegetables are softened.
4. Add minced garlic to the pot and cook for 1 minute, until fragrant.
5. Return the browned chicken pieces to the pot. Pour in chicken broth and add bay leaf, dried thyme, dried parsley, dried rosemary, and dried sage (if using). Bring to a boil, then reduce heat to low and simmer, covered, for about 45 minutes to 1 hour, or until the chicken is cooked through and tender.

6. While the chicken is simmering, prepare the dumplings. In a bowl, whisk together flour, baking powder, salt, and black pepper. Cut in cold butter using a pastry cutter or fork until the mixture resembles coarse crumbs. Stir in milk until just combined, being careful not to overmix.
7. Once the chicken is cooked through and tender, remove it from the pot and set aside to cool slightly. Discard the bay leaf.
8. Increase the heat to medium-high. Drop spoonfuls of the dumpling batter into the simmering broth. Cover and cook for 15-20 minutes, or until the dumplings are cooked through and fluffy.
9. While the dumplings are cooking, shred the cooked chicken meat into bite-sized pieces, discarding the bones and skin.
10. Stir in frozen peas (if using) and heavy cream (if using) into the pot. Return the shredded chicken to the pot and cook for another 5 minutes, until heated through. Adjust seasoning with salt and pepper to taste.
11. Serve the chicken and dumplings hot, garnished with chopped fresh parsley if desired.

Chicken and dumplings is a comforting and satisfying dish perfect for colder days or anytime you need a hearty meal. Enjoy the tender chicken, fluffy dumplings, and flavorful broth!

Beef lasagna

Ingredients:

For the meat sauce:

- 1 pound (450g) lean ground beef
- 1 onion, chopped
- 4 cloves garlic, minced
- 1 can (28 ounces) crushed tomatoes
- 1 can (6 ounces) tomato paste
- 1/2 cup water or beef broth
- 2 teaspoons dried oregano
- 2 teaspoons dried basil
- 1 teaspoon salt, or to taste
- 1/2 teaspoon black pepper, or to taste

For the cheese filling:

- 15 ounces (about 2 cups) ricotta cheese
- 1 cup grated Parmesan cheese
- 1 large egg
- 2 tablespoons chopped fresh parsley (optional)
- Salt and pepper, to taste

Other ingredients:

- 12 lasagna noodles, cooked according to package instructions (or use no-boil lasagna noodles)
- 2 cups shredded mozzarella cheese
- Additional grated Parmesan cheese, for topping

Instructions:

1. Preheat your oven to 375°F (190°C). Lightly grease a 9x13-inch baking dish.
2. In a large skillet or Dutch oven, cook the ground beef over medium-high heat until browned and cooked through. Drain any excess fat.
3. Add chopped onion to the skillet and cook for 5 minutes, until softened. Add minced garlic and cook for 1 minute more.
4. Stir in crushed tomatoes, tomato paste, water or beef broth, dried oregano, dried basil, salt, and black pepper. Bring to a simmer and cook for 15-20 minutes, stirring occasionally, until the sauce thickens slightly. Taste and adjust seasoning as needed. Remove from heat.
5. In a medium bowl, combine ricotta cheese, grated Parmesan cheese, egg, chopped parsley (if using), salt, and pepper. Mix until well combined.

6. To assemble the lasagna, spread a thin layer of meat sauce on the bottom of the prepared baking dish.
7. Arrange a single layer of cooked lasagna noodles over the sauce, overlapping slightly to cover the bottom of the dish.
8. Spread half of the ricotta cheese mixture evenly over the noodles.
9. Spoon about one-third of the remaining meat sauce over the ricotta layer, spreading it out evenly.
10. Sprinkle about one-third of the shredded mozzarella cheese over the meat sauce.
11. Repeat with another layer of noodles, the remaining ricotta cheese mixture, another third of the meat sauce, and another third of the shredded mozzarella cheese.
12. Finish with a final layer of noodles, the remaining meat sauce, and the remaining shredded mozzarella cheese.
13. Sprinkle additional grated Parmesan cheese over the top.
14. Cover the baking dish loosely with aluminum foil, tenting it slightly to prevent it from touching the cheese.
15. Bake in the preheated oven for 30 minutes. Remove the foil and bake for an additional 15-20 minutes, or until the lasagna is hot and bubbly, and the cheese is melted and lightly browned.
16. Remove from the oven and let it cool for 10 minutes before slicing and serving.

Beef lasagna is best served warm, allowing the layers to set slightly for easier slicing. Serve with a side of garlic bread and a green salad for a complete meal. Enjoy the delicious flavors of this classic Italian comfort food!

Cauliflower cheese

Ingredients:

- 1 large head of cauliflower, cut into florets
- 2 tablespoons unsalted butter
- 2 tablespoons all-purpose flour
- 1 1/2 cups milk
- 1 cup grated cheddar cheese (or any melting cheese of your choice)
- 1/4 teaspoon ground nutmeg
- Salt and pepper, to taste
- 1/4 cup breadcrumbs (optional, for topping)
- Fresh parsley, chopped (optional, for garnish)

Instructions:

1. Preheat your oven to 375°F (190°C). Butter a 2-quart baking dish or casserole dish.
2. Bring a large pot of salted water to a boil. Add the cauliflower florets and cook for about 5 minutes, or until just tender. Drain well and set aside.
3. In a medium saucepan, melt the butter over medium heat. Add the flour and whisk constantly for 1-2 minutes to make a roux.
4. Gradually whisk in the milk, a little at a time, until smooth and thickened. Cook for 3-4 minutes, stirring frequently, until the sauce coats the back of a spoon.
5. Remove the saucepan from heat and stir in grated cheddar cheese until melted and smooth. Season with ground nutmeg, salt, and pepper to taste.
6. Add the cooked cauliflower florets to the cheese sauce and gently stir to coat evenly.
7. Transfer the cauliflower mixture to the prepared baking dish, spreading it out evenly.
8. If using breadcrumbs, sprinkle them evenly over the cauliflower cheese mixture.
9. Bake in the preheated oven for 20-25 minutes, or until the top is golden brown and bubbly.
10. Remove from the oven and let it cool for a few minutes before serving.
11. Garnish with chopped fresh parsley, if desired, and serve hot as a delicious side dish or a vegetarian main course.

Cauliflower cheese is creamy, cheesy, and full of flavor, making it a favorite comfort food that pairs well with roasted meats, grilled chicken, or as part of a holiday feast. Enjoy this simple and satisfying dish!